RIPARIAN AREA MANAGEMENT

Inventory and Monitoring Riparian Areas

by

Lewis H. Myers
Wildlife Biologist
Bureau of Land Management
Dillon Resource Area, Montana

Technical Reference 1737-3
July 1989

U.S. Department of the Interior
Bureau of Land Management
Service Center
P.O. Box 25047
Denver CO 80225-0047

Acknowledgment

The following BLM personnel contributed significantly to completion of this reference document, and their input is appreciated

Al Amen, SC
Ray Boyd, SC
Allen Cooperrider, SC
Kris Eshelman, SC
Karl Gebhardt, Idaho SO
Don Prichard, SC
Robert Wagner, SC
John Willoughby, California SO
Bruce Van Haveren, SC

Table of Contents

List of Figures

List of Tables

Inventory and Monitoring Riparian Areas

1. Purpose

1.1 Use of Riparian Inventory and Monitoring Data

Site data play an important role in providing a baseline from which to:

(1) Describe present riparian vegetation.

(2) Determine the approximate potential and ecological status of a riparian site.

(3) Establish a resource value rating for a particular use or benefit.

(4) Provide a reference point for establishing management objectives from which to monitor.

(5) Predict acceptable use levels (e.g., aesthetic, watershed, wildlife and fish, livestock) that would result from alternative management strategies.

(6) Meet the inventory requirements addressed in the Federal Land Policy and Management Act of 1976, the Public Rangelands Improvement Act of 1978, and Bureau of Land Management Policy.

1.2 Inventory and Monitoring Strategy

This Technical Reference (TR) contains suggested techniques and procedures. It will assist managers in determining their specific inventory and monitoring needs. Inventory components are shown as essential or optional. Essential components should be emphasized, but they are not required. Optional components should receive less emphasis, but they may be required to meet specific management needs.

The approach to inventory and monitoring is shown in Figure 1. The extensive inventory is completed using primarily remote sensing, maps, existing data, and limited field analysis. With extensive inventory data, managers identify, characterize, and roughly classify riparian sites. A decision can then be made on priorities for intensive inventories based on resource values and site characters. Low resorce values and/or acceptable condition may dictate the development of maintenance objectives and the establishment of monitoring without the completion of an intensive inventory. High values and/or unacceptable condition would probably result in a decision to do an intensive inventory.

In other cases, the extensive inventory may be inconclusive and the cost of an intensive inventory may not be justified. Managers may then proceed with a supplement to the extensive inventory consisting of a field analysis of three attributes. This additional riparian condition data should allow managers to decide if an intensive inventory is warranted.

Intensive inventories require detailed field examination. These data are used to classify sites in more detail, and to provide site-specific management objectives and monitoring criteria.

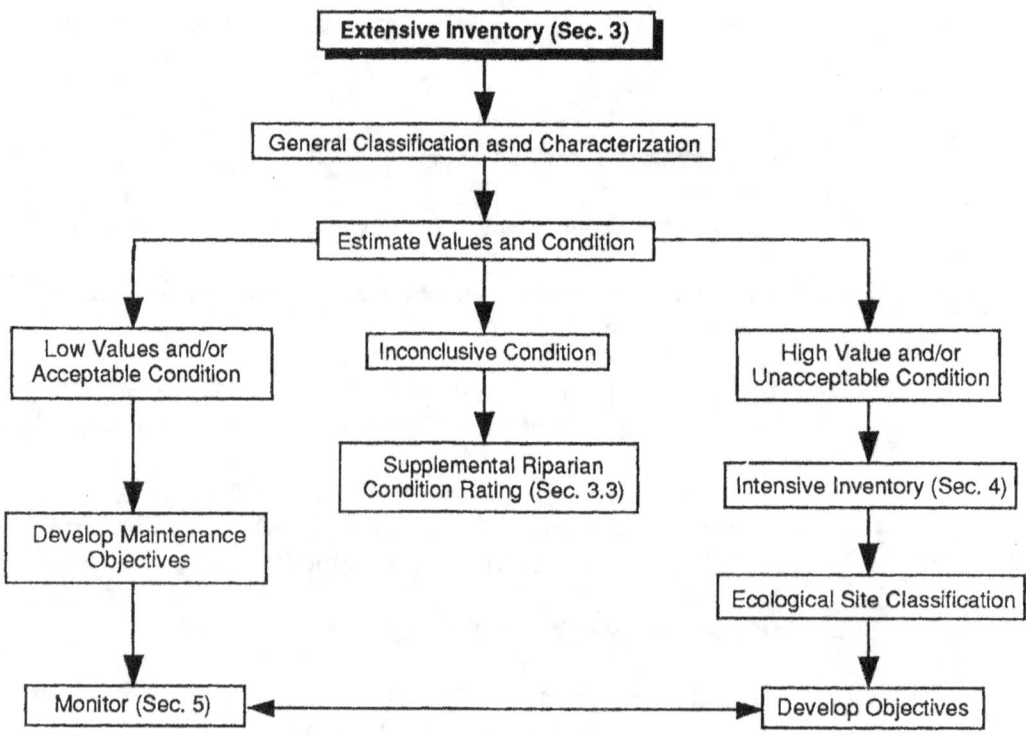

Figure 1. Riparian Inventory, Classification and Monitoring Strategy.

1.3 Application of Technical Reference

Emphasis is placed on inventory and monitoring of riverine riparian sites. Application to springs, wet meadows, ponds and lakes may require some adaptation.

2. Coordination

Riparian areas are unique and among the most productive and important ecosystems. Although comprising only a small percentage of the public lands, they affect most other resources and values. Given the high value of these areas for a variety of resources, all aspects of riparian area inventory, monitoring, and management will comprise a multidisciplinary effort, with input by range, wildlife, and soils-hydrology staffs, at a minimum. Where applicable, coordination may also be required with recreation and forestry Specialists. State and other federal agencies and interested public user groups should also be consulted.

3. Extensive Inventory

3.1 General Considerations

3.11 Scope and Essential Components

The primary purpose of an extensive inventory is to locate, quantify, and broadly classify riparian ecological sites. Inventory data can be used as reference material in documents of general scope and as a planning tool for identifying and prioritizing intensive inventory needs. Ideally, an extensive inventory should be completed on all Bureau lands prior to initiation of intensive inventories.

Emphasis is placed upon use of existing aerial photography and USGS quadrangle maps, with little or no ground-truthing. Field assessment is required for soil characters. Where applicable, a supplemental field assessment of riparian condition may be needed. (see 1.2, 3.3)

The basic tools consist of small-scale aerial photos (1:15,000 to 1:30,000) and USGS quad maps (1:24,000). Large-scale photography (1:4,000 or larger), when available, allows for more refined descriptions of inventory features. Contracts for low-level color or CIR photography may be an efficient means of completing an extensive inventory. Cuplin et al. (1985) have identified variables that may be interpreted from large-scale aerial photography. TR 1737-2 (Batson, et al. 1987) demonstrates the use of large scale IR photography for inventorying and monitoring riparian areas.

The described components are considered minimal and essential to an extensive inventory of riparian areas. Additional information should be collected depending upon local management objectives and specific requirements. For example, a riparian area being evaluated with a management objective to provide nesting habitat for a threatened or endangered (T/E) raptor species should include observations on present or potential nest sites (trees, etc.) and availability of a prey base.

3.12 Environmental Influences

Many environmental factors affect riparian vegetation succession, and some are not influenced by management practices. Inventories should include a written record of influencing factors.

Climate and biogeography ultimately play a critical role in species composition of floodplain communities (Brinson, et al., 1981). Riparian communities are probably the most dynamic of any ecosystem. An excellent review of riparian ecosystem functions is provided by Brinson et al. (1981).

3.13 Soils

Soils occurring within riparian areas are extremely variable in texture, depth, degree of wetness, and rock fragment content because they are forming in mixed, alluvial materials derived from a variety of sources and parent rock. The general soil setting information is difficult to inventory and describe because

(1) they are variable within short distances;

(2) they commonly occur in intricate, micro-relief patterns as small, narrow, elongated areas; and

(3) in many instances they cannot be delineated on 1:24,000-scale maps.

Where no detailed soil survey information is available, general soil setting information can be obtained from aerial photograph interpretations, USGS Quadrangle maps, climatic data, geologic data, and review of county general soils maps showing soils adjoining riparian areas. This information should be supplemented by field observations at selected sites. The number and location of selected sites for field observations will depend on the complexity of the area sampled. Site selection would be based on the general soil setting, available related resource information (geology and vegetation), and aerial photographic interpretations. This would be considered a schematic soil inventory in that kinds of soils and the areas in which they occur would be predicted mainly from existing information and limited field observations without the benefit of detailed field investigations. County soils maps will provide only a general view of the soils within the surrounding area.

Where detailed soil surveys are available (mainly order 3), some of the riparian areas may not be delineated due to the scale of maps and the small size of the area. This would require inference of soil information from the adjoining soil map units and additional field observations. Most riparian areas mapped are identified as complexes, associations, or undifferentiated map units because of the intricate and complex occurrence of soils within riparian areas. Information from these map units will provide an adequate extensive soil inventory.

3.14 Riparian Ecological Site

A riparian ecological site is a specific kind of potential riparian association within the riparian ecosystem. It is synonymous with range site (USDA 1976) and ecological site (USDI 1981).

A riparian ecosystem is the transitional area between the aquatic ecosystem and terrestrial ecosystem, identified by soil characteristics and distinctive vegetation communities that require free or unbound water (USDI 1985a). Climatic, physiographic, and particularly groundwater/surface water functions play a greater role than soils and precipitation in determining floristic composition of riparian associations. Though less extrapolative emphasis may be placed on soils and precipitation in identifying potential of riparian sites, as opposed to upland sites, the concept of ecological site is applicable.

4

An ecological site is a kind of land which differs from other kinds of land in its potential natural community and physical site characteristics, and thus also differs in its ability to produce vegetation and its response to management (Range Inventory and Standardization Committee, 1983).

Riparian sites will be described using criteria in BLM Manual Handbook H-4410-1.

3.2 Extensive Inventory Procedures

3.21 Basin Components

(a) **Drainage Pattern.** The pattern is portrayed by a planar projection of the watershed on a map (Figure 2). This information is used subjectively to determine hydrologic response to precipitation. Elongated basins with a trellis drainage pattern often occur in folded terrain where the various rock strata have differing resistance to weathering. Circular basins with a more dendritic drainage pattern occur where the bedrock is more horizontal and homogeneous. Record drainages as type a, b, or c.

(b) **Basin Elevation Range.** Record the lowest elevation on the stream segment and the highest elevation within the stream segment basin.

3.22 Segment Components

(a) **Landform.** Determine landform from maps and photos using the classifications referred to in the Riparian Aquatic Inventory Data Summary (RAIDS) data base.

(b) **Elevation, Upstream and Downstream.** Determine elevations at upper and lower extremes of riparian Site Writeup Area (SWA) from contours of large-scale topographic maps or with field altimeter readings.

(c) **Drainage Area.** The watershed area (acres) contributing runoff to a given point on a stream. It includes all drainage area upstream from the most downstream part of the segment.

(d) **Orientation.** The mean compass direction that the stream segment faces.

(e) **Stream Order.** First-order streams are unbranched reaches found usually, but not exclusively, at the head of drainage basins (Figure 3). Second-order streams are formed by the confluence of two or more first order streams. First-order streams must have an identifiable channel, but need not be perennial. Determine the stream order from maps and photos using the technique of Boehne and House (1983). Additional details are presented in Helm (1985).

5

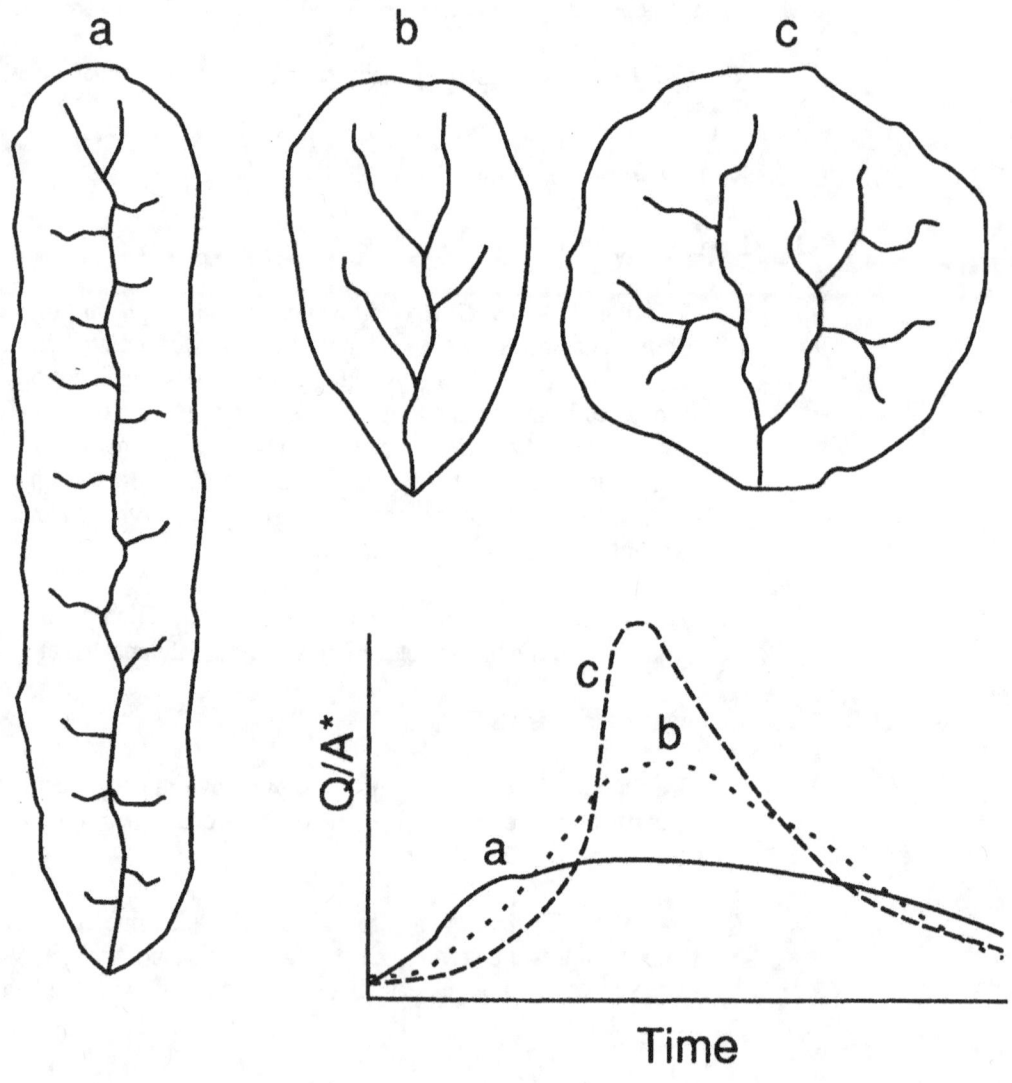

* Stream discharge per unit of watershed area

Figure 2. Some common drainage patterns and their representative rainfall-runoff hydrographs.

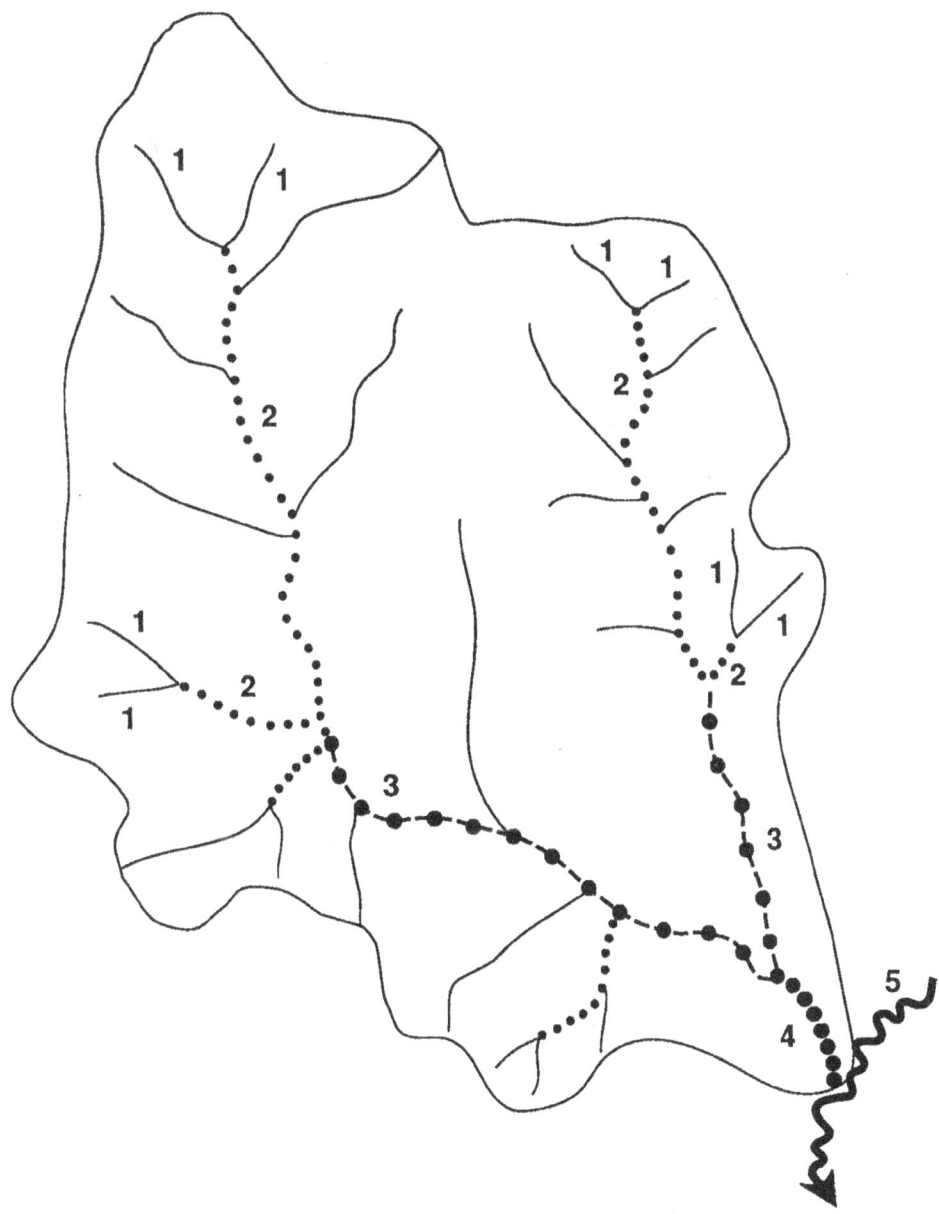

Figure 3. Stream ordering system for a watershed. First-order streams are unbranched reaches, which when combined form a second-order stream; two second-order streams form a third-order stream.

(f) **Soil Texture Class, Rock Fragment Modifier and Stoniness Class.** An outline of acceptable general terms (USDA, 1981) in three classes and in five classes in relation to the basic soil textural classes names is shown as follows:

General Terms	Texture	Basic Soil Textural Class Names
Sandy Soils	Coarse-textured	Sand Loamy sands
	Moderately coarse-textured	Sandy loam Fine sandy loam
Loamy Soils	Medium-textured	Very fine sandy loam Loam Silt Loam Silt
	Moderately fine-textured	Clay loam Sandy clay loam Silty clay loam
Clayey Soils	Fine-textured	Sandy clay Silty clay Clay

Textural classes would be modified by the addition of suitable adjectives where rock fragments (larger than 0.08 in.) such as gravel, cobble, stones or boulders are present in substantial amounts (greater than 15 percent by volume). Refer to Soil Survey Manual (USDA, 1981) for terms and parameters.

Stoniness refers to the relative portions of rock fragments 10 inches to 24 inches (25 cm to 60 cm) in diameter in and on the soil. Boulders are more than 24 inches (60 cm) in diameter. Refer to Soil Survey Manual (USDA, 1981) for definition of classes.

Only the presence (not classes) of rock fragments will be identified in extensive inventory, e.g., gravelly, cobbly, stony, or bouldery.

(g) **General Soil Water (Wetness).** This is one of the most important soil properties in riparian ecological site classification in that it strongly influences the type of vegetation. General degree and duration of wetness would be described. Phases of soil wetness recognized for the extensive inventory are wet (including somewhat poorly drained, poorly drained, very poorly drained soils) and drained soils. Refer to Soil Survey Manual (USDA, 1981) for definitions.

(h) **General Soil Reaction.** Soil alkalinity is an important soil property affecting plant composition, plant growth, soil use, and management. The degree of alkalinity or acidity in a soil is expressed by pH values and associated terminology. Refer to Soil Survey Manual (USDA, 1981) for determining degrees of soil reaction. For the extensive inventory identify soils as alkaline where pH exceeds 8.4 and as acidic where pH is less than 6.0.

(i) **General Soil Salinity.** Salinity phases are used to distinguish between degrees of salinity that are important for soil use and management within the range of a soil series or taxon of a higher category. The observed plant type and growth are evidence for recognizing salinity. Degrees of salinity identified for the extensive inventory are saline and non-saline. Refer to Soil Survey Manual (USDA, 1981) for determining degrees of salinity.

(j) **Channel Gradient.** Gradient is an easy attribute to measure. First, determine the upper and lower elevations, then measure the length of the stream channel using a planimeter or other map-measuring device; being careful to account for meander. Gradient (in percent) is the elevation difference divided by the channel length (in hundreds of feet). However, this measurement may not be accurate in entrenched or incised systems. Generally, gradient is estimated from a map, measured by an instrument.

(k) **Channel Sinuosity.** Sinuosity is a commonly used attribute in classifying rivers. It is the ratio of stream length between two points divided by the valley length between the same two points (Figure 4). Experience in the field suggest using a sufficiently long stream reach (Platts et al. 1983). In their investigations, they used a distance of 20 times the channel width. For the extensive inventory a 7.5 minute quadrangle map or aerial photograph should be used to make these determinations.

(l) **Channel Confinement.** Confinement is the relation of channel to the valley walls. Kellerhals, Church, and Bray (1976) list four types of relations as:

   (1) occasionally confined; river is occasionally deflected by the valley wall or a resistant terrace (Figure 5),

   (2) frequently confined (Figure 5),

   (3) confined; the river is frequently deflected by the valley walls or terraces (Figure 6), and

   (4) entrenched; also continuously confined (Figure 7).

(m) **Channel Entrenchment.** Entrenchment i.e., downcutting, is the relation of channel to valley flat. Kellerhals, Church, and Bray (1976) list four types of relations as:

   (1) Aggrading; typified by deltaic and braided reaches filling the entire valley,

   (2) not obviously degrading or aggrading,

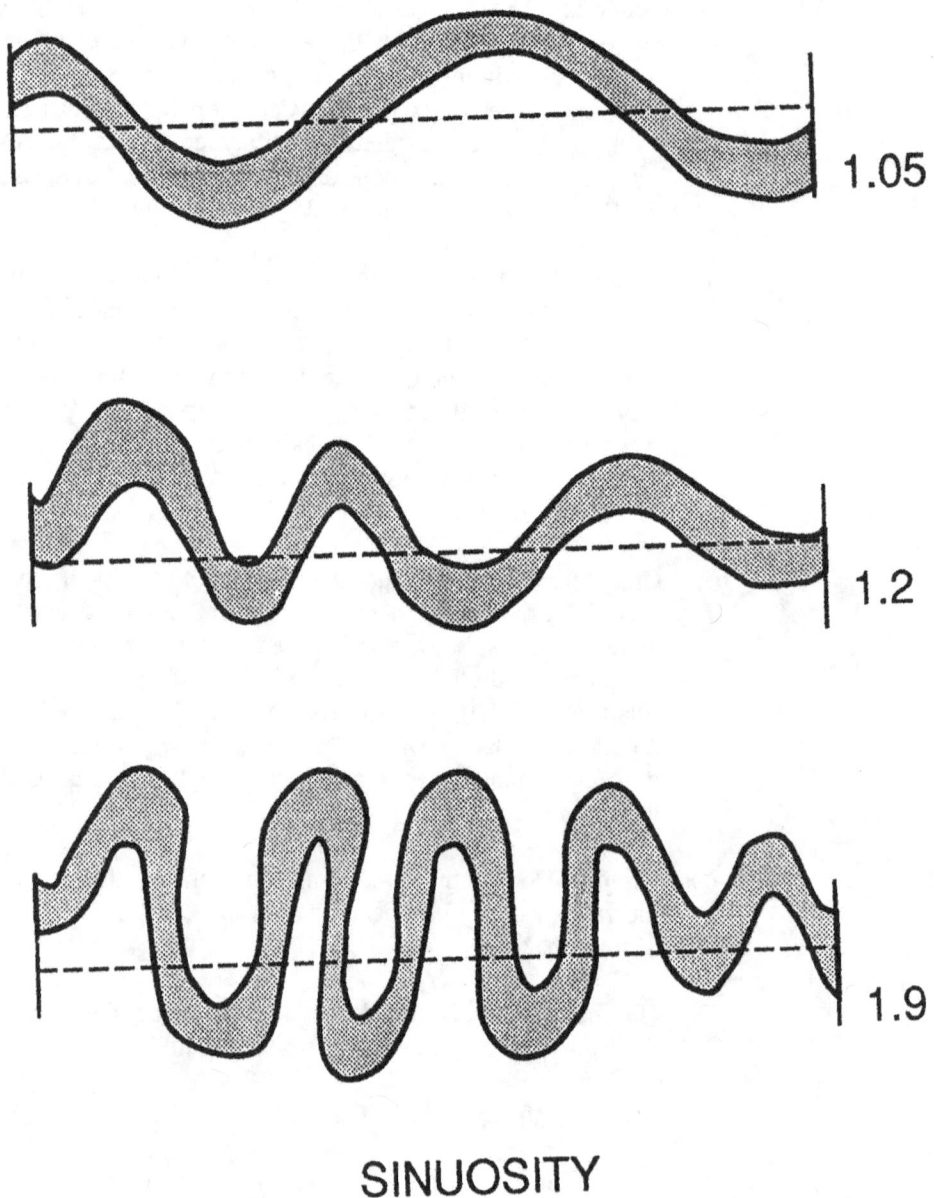

1.05

1.2

1.9

SINUOSITY

Figure 4. Illustrations of stream sinuosity, or the ratio of stream length divided by the valley length between two points. Sinuosity ratios are shown on the right.

10

OCCASIONALLY CONFINED

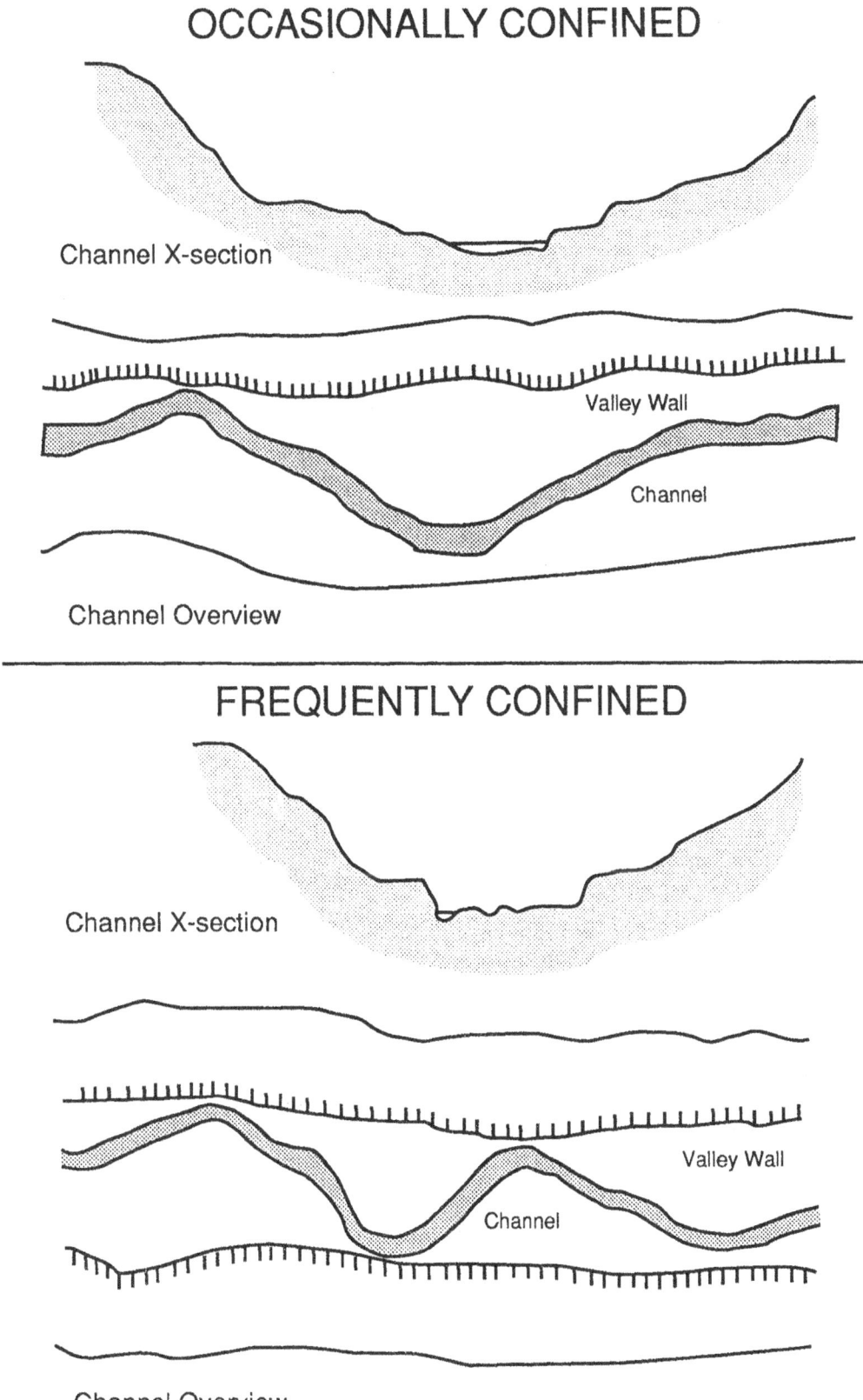

Channel X-section

Valley Wall

Channel

Channel Overview

FREQUENTLY CONFINED

Channel X-section

Valley Wall

Channel

Channel Overview

Figure 5. Occasionally and frequently confined channels.

CONFINED

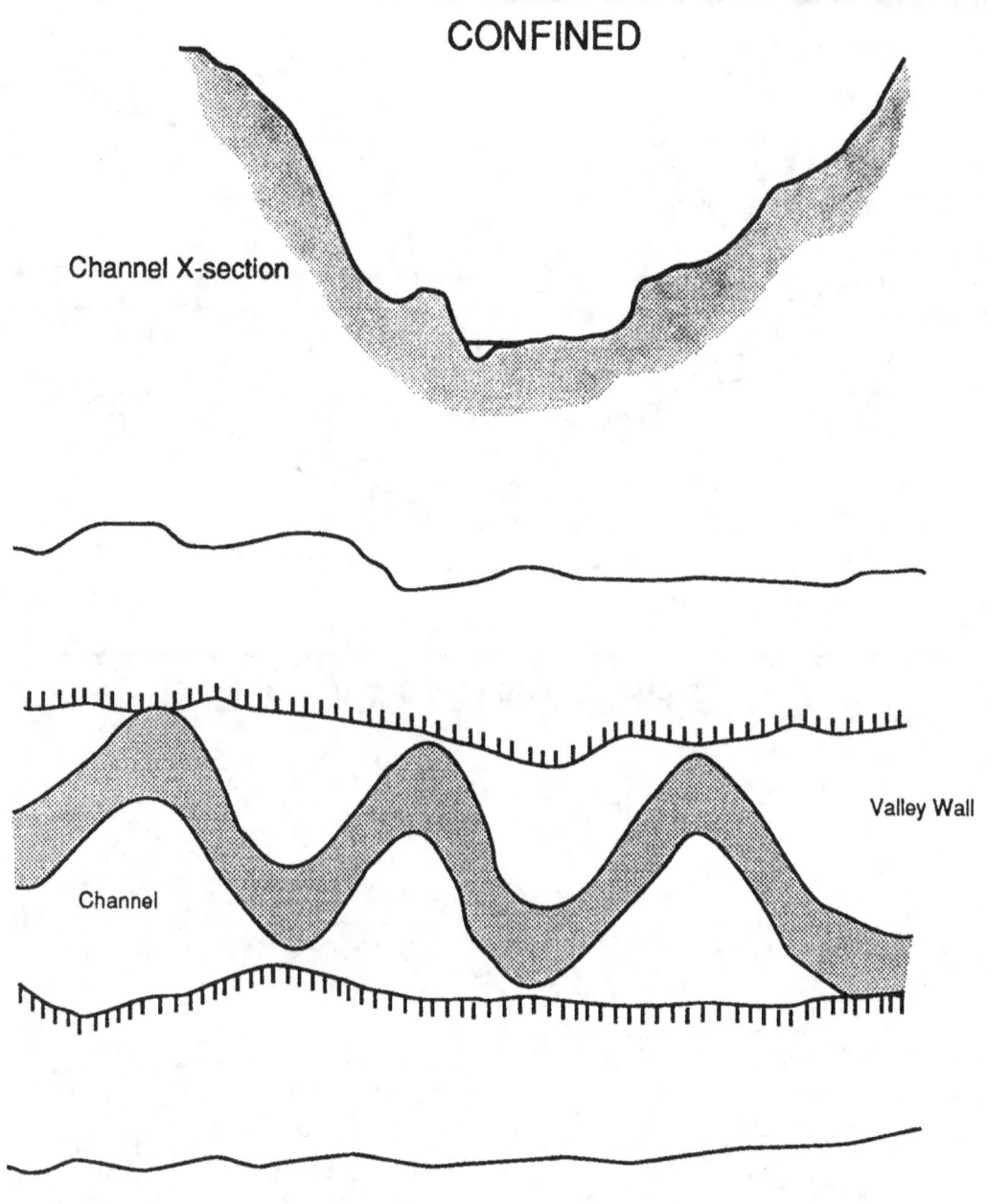

Figure 6. Channel confinement.

12

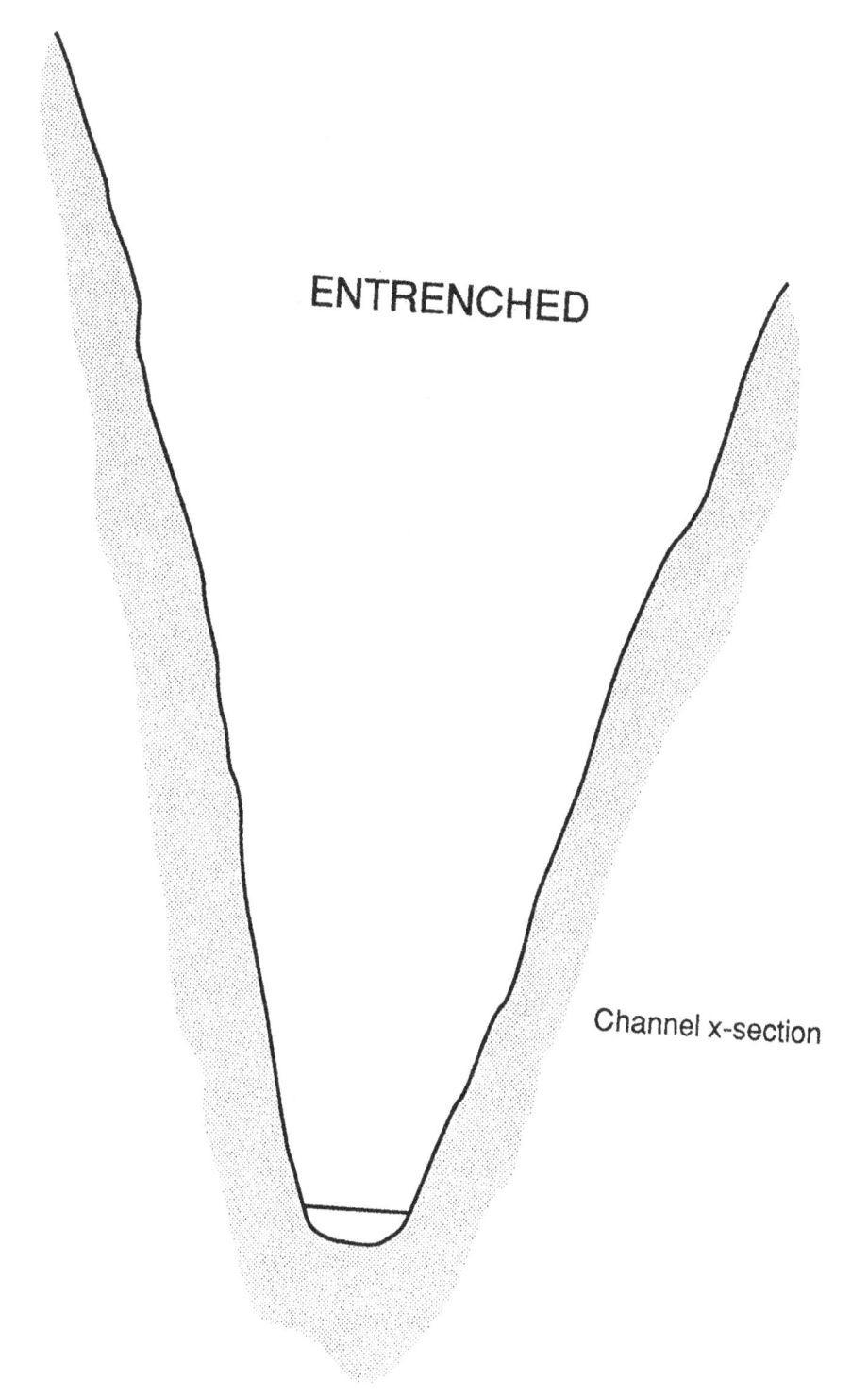

ENTRENCHED

Channel x-section

Figure 7. Entrenched channel.

(3) partly entrenched, and,

(4) entrenched (Figure 7).

(n) **Channel Lateral Movement.** Kellerhals, Church, and Bray (1976) used this attribute to describe the predominant type of lateral channel activity in the reach. Select one of the following:

(1) Not evident. No evidence of much past channel movement, typical of a confined system.

(2) Avulsion. Channel has evidence (detectable in aerial photo's) of dramatic movement from its present location (Figure 8). This should not be confused with a braided channel although braiding may be occurring on parts of the stream.

(3) Downcutting and Widening. Stream has undergone severe downcutting resulting from headcutting and gullying processes and is now beginning to meander from side to side resulting in channel widening (Figure 8).

(4) Progression. Channel shows a progressive lateral movement particularly at the meanders. The channel does not appear to get wider because of deposition on the bank opposite the eroding bank.

(o) **Streamflow Duration.** Duration is the flow regime describing the basic behavior of seasonal flows. Rosgen (1985) describes flow regime in four classes:

(1) Ephemeral. Flows only in response to precipitation.

(2) Subterranean. Flows parallel to and near the surface for various seasons; a sub-surface flow which follows the stream channel bed.

(3) Intermittent. One which flows seasonally or sporadically. Surface sources involve springs, snow melt, artificial controls, etc.

(4) Perennial. Surface water persists year-long.

(p) **Streamflow.** Record typical low flow and high flow, as a minimum, if known. Additional data may be recorded if available.

(q) **Streamflow Regulation.** Regulation is an additional modifier to variation for categorizing the largest influence on flow. Examples would be reservoir, spring-fed, groundwater control, etc.

(r) **Vegetation Series.** The series is defined by the dominant species or set of species in the overstory. Generally, stereoscopic photo interpretation will permit identification of the existing dominant

14

AVULSION (overview)

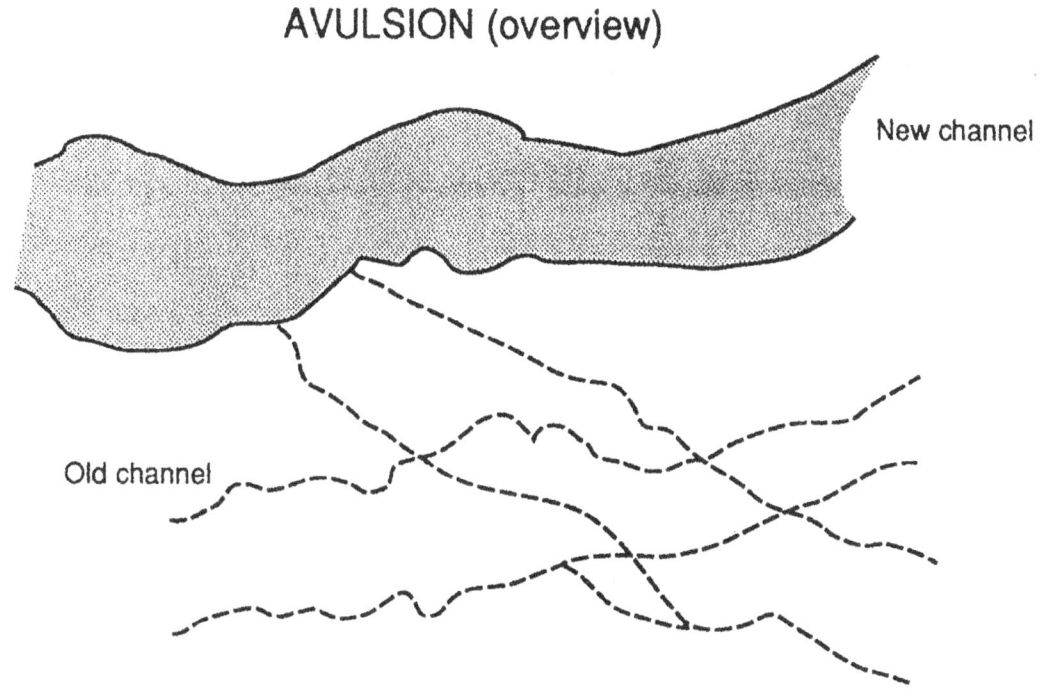

New channel

Old channel

DOWNCUT AND WIDEN (overview)

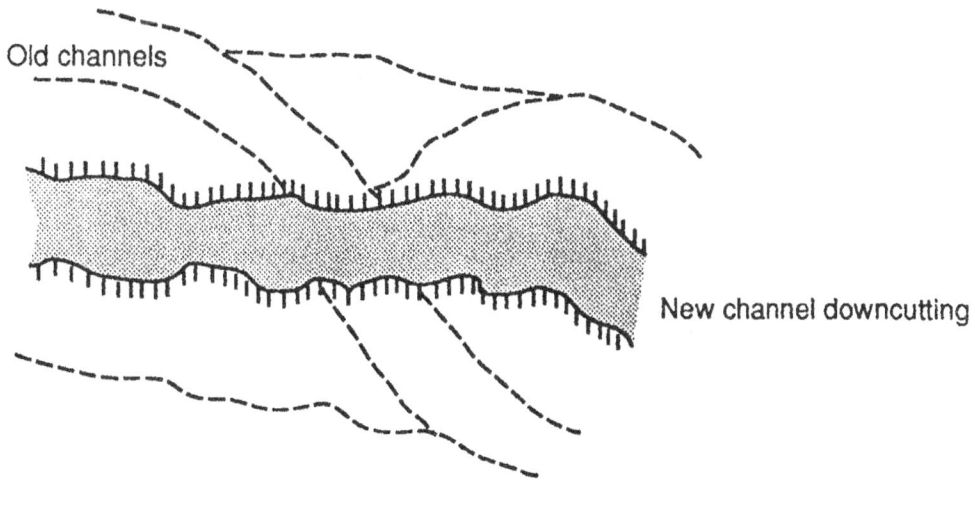

Old channels

New channel downcutting

Figure 8. Channel movement, showing avulsion of downcut; lateral characters.

15

nant overstory species. Comparison of physiographic features with known series on similar sites will aid photo interpretation. Dominance is determined by aerial crown-cover. Experienced field personnel will generally recognize dominants to the species level. Associations characterized by species which are ecologically homologous and within the same genus, may be named by genus, e.g., *Salix* series. Limited ground-truthing may be required on some sites where the dominant layer is herbaceous, or where codominance occurs in overstory cover.

(s) **Ecological Site/SWA.** Stereoscopic photo interpretation, along with physiographic analysis of a quadrangle map, should allow preliminary ecological typing (Section 4.14). This will generally coincide with obvious vegetation series and/or physical site change. Dividing drainages into landform zones such as boulder, floodway, and pastoral (Bowers et al., 1979) may be useful. Within the broad zones, ecological sites may vary as a result of flow regime, gradient, or climatic extremes. Tentative ecological site boundaries should be shown on maps/photos pending refinement through ground-truthing or an intensive inventory.

Tentative SWA boundaries corresponding to ecological site boundaries, present vegetation communities, and fences and administrative boundaries should be mapped and numbered. A SWA will not extend beyond a fence although an ecological site can.

(t) **Valley Width.** General width of the valley from a contour map as evidenced by change in slope (contour intervals). In mountains it will be very narrow. Width can be estimated in hundreds of feet.

(u) **Cross-Valley Slope.** The general side-slope across the valley towards the stream center, expressed as percent, can be measured from a contour map.

3.3   Supplemental Riparian Condition Rating

3.31   Purpose and Definitions

Managers may not have the capability or need to complete intensive inventories on all riparian areas. An option is to supplement the extensive inventory by making systematic ocular assessments of three riparian site attributes (bank alteration, veg. bank protection, and subsurface water status). This rating assists the manager in prioritizing management and/or intensive inventory needs.

This procedure is independent of resource value ratings. It considers only riparian site function and does not address the causes of riparian site degradation.

16

Riparian sites are shallow aquifers which recharge at peak flows and discharge at normal and low flows. The shallow aquifer supports plant communities which are a stabilizing force and which facilitate deposition of fluvial sediments at high flows.

Van Haveren and Jackson (1986) discuss hydrologic and geomorphic processes, and their interrelationships with the stream-dependent water table. The three rating attributes, bank alteration, vegetative bank protection, and subsurface water status are interdependent. When the fluvial deposition process is impaired due to loss of vegetation cover, increased channel or bank erosion ensues, reducing flood plain recharge and further stressing water table dependent plants.

Use of existing data elements acquired through other inventory or monitoring efforts is encouraged and may substantially reduce the effort of data collection used for this assessment.

3.32   Rating Attributes

Three rating attributes are described below. These can be modified as required to reflect regional conditions. Other attributes may also be added.

(a)   **Streambank Soil Alteration** (from Platts et al. 1987) Certain land uses, especially livestock grazing, can start the modification of a stream by causing instability of the bank. This streambank alteration rating, therefore, may provide a warning system for changes indicative of site deterioration.

The rating is separated into four classes (Table 1). Each class, except the one with no alteration, has an evaluation spread of 25 percentage points. Once the class is determined, the observer must decide the actual percent of instability. Streambanks are evaluated on the basis of how far they have moved away from optimum conditions for the respective habitat type. Therefore, the observer must be able to visualize the streambank as it would appear under optimum conditions.

Table 1. Streambank Soil Alteration Rating

Rating Value	Percent	Description
4	0	Streambanks are stable and are not being altered by water flows or animals.
	1 to 25	Streambanks are stable, but are being lightly altered along the transect line. Less than 25 percent of the streambank is receiving any kind of stress, and if stress is being received, it is very light. Less than 25 percent of the streambank is false,* broken down, or eroding.
3	26 to 50	Streambanks are receiving only moderate alteration along the transect line. At least 50 percent of the streambank is in a natural stable condition. Less than 50 percent of the streambank is false*, broken down, or eroding. False banks are rated as altered. Alteration is rated as natural, artificial, or a combination of the two.
2	51 to 75	Streambanks have received major alteration along the transect line. Less than 50 percent of the streambank is in a stable condition. Over 50 percent of the streambank is false*, broken down, or eroding. A false bank that may have gained some stability and cover is still rated as altered. Alteration is rated as natural, artificial, or a combination of the two.
1	76 to 100	Streambanks along the transect line are severely altered. Less than 25 percent of the streambank is in a stable condition. Over 75 percent of the streambank is false,* broken down, or eroding. A past damaged bank, now classified as a false bank, that has gained some stability and cover is still rated as altered. Alteration is rated as natural, artificial, or a combination of the two.

False banks are those banks which have been cut back by cattle and are no longer immediately adjacent to the stream.

Any natural or artificial alteration deviating from this optimum condition is included in the valuation. This visualization makes uniformity in rating an alteration difficult, because it is difficult to train all observers to visualize the same optimum bank condition. Natural alteration is any change in the bank produced by natural events. Artificial alteration is any change obviously produced by exotic force. Trampling by man or livestock, disturbance by bulldozers, etc., are examples of artificial changes. Natural and artificial alterations are reported individually, but together they cannot exceed 100 percent. It is often difficult to distinguish artificial from natural alterations; if there is any doubt, the alteration is classified as natural. It is possible to have artificial alterations cover already existing natural alterations and vice-versa. Only the major type of alteration on a unit area enters the rating system in this case.

Platts et al. 1983, recommends rating only that part of streambanks intercepted by channel cross-section transects. Rating of entire banks increased observer error. The number of temporary cross section samples required will vary with channel consistency, and should be determined in the field using a coefficient of variation analysis (Eshelman et al., 1986). This can quickly be done on a pocket calculator with standard deviation function.

(b)   **Vegetative Bank Protection** Pfankuch (1975) developed rating factors for vegetation vigor and structure in USFS Region One (Table 2). A tree/shrub dominance is assumed, thus these criteria may require modification to account for inherent regional differences. Modification necessitates some knowledge of site potential.

The soil in banks is held in place largely by plant roots. Riparian plants have almost unlimited water for both crown and root development. Their root mats generally increase in density with proximity to the open channel. Trees and shrubs generally have deeper root systems than grasses and forbs. Roots seldom extend far into the water table, however, and near the shore of lakes and streams they may be comparatively shallow rooted. Some species are, therefore, subject to windthrow.

In addition to the benefits of the root mat in stabilizing the banks, the stems help to reduce the velocity of flood flows. Turbulence is generated by stems in what may have been laminar flow. The seriousness of this energy release depends on the density of both overstory and understory vegetation. The greater the density of both, the more resistance displayed. Damage from turbulence is greatest at the periphery and diminishes with distance from the normal channel. Other factors to consider, in addition to the density of stems, are the varieties of vegetation, the vigor of growth and the reproduction processes. Vegetal variety is more desirable than a monotypic plant community. Young plants, growing and reproducing vigorously, are better than old, decadent stands.

Table 2. Vegetative Bank Protection

Rating Value	Description
4	**Excellent:** Trees, shrubs, grass, and forbs combined cover more than 90 percent of the ground. Openings in this nearly complete cover are small and evenly dispersed. A variety of species and age classes are represented. Growth is vigorous and reproduction of species in both the under and overstory is proceeding at a rate to insure continued ground cover conditions. A deep, dense root mat is inferred.
3	**Good:** Plants cover 70 to 90 percent of the ground. Shrub species are more prevalent than trees. Openings in the tree canopy are larger than the space resulting from the loss of a single mature individual. While the growth vigor is generally good for all species, advanced reproduction may be sparse or lacking entirely. A deep root mat is not continuous and more serious erosive incursions can occur in the openings.
2	**Fair:** Plant cover ranges from 50 to 70 percent. Lack of vigor is evident in some individuals and/or species. Seedling reproduction is nil. This condition ranked fair, based mostly on the percent of the area not covered by vegetation with a deep root mat potential and less on the kind of plants that make up the overstory.
1	**Poor:** Less than 50 percent of the ground is covered. Trees are essentially absent. Shrubs largely exist in scattered clumps. Growth and reproduction vigor are generally poor. Root mats are discontinuous and shallow.

(c) **Subsurface Water Status.** This attribute utilizes the status of hydrophytic plants as a general indicator of shallow aquifer status (Table 3). Hydrophytes are plants growing in water or on a substrate that is at least periodically deficient in oxygen as a result of excessive water content (USDA, 1985). Hydrophytic plant lists are provided by the Wetland Ecology Group (USDI, 1986) for various regions (Appendix 1). For purposes of this rating, hydrophytes will comprise, obligate, and facilitate wetland species as defined by the wetland ecology group and as consistent with interpretations of the Soil Conservation Service. Upland plants include all species which do not meet the hydrophyte criteria.

Where site deterioration occurs, accompanied by lateral erosion or channel incision, the recharge function is impaired, and the riparian site aquifer level is lowered, becoming less available to hydrophytic plants. In extreme cases, upland plant species which are intolerant to saturated soils may dominate former riparian sites.

This attribute also indirectly measures the influence of grazing. Adverse grazing practices reduce the vigor of palatable plants, which reduces riparian site stability, contributing to channel incision or lateral erosion and loss of aquifer recharge/discharge function.

20

Table 3. Subsurface Water Status

Rating Value	Description
4	Riparian site vegetation composition dominated by hydrophytic plants; reproduction evident. Little or no encroachment of upland plants (plants intolerant to prolonged saturated soil). Upland plants limited largely to the riparian/upland interface.
3	Riparian site vegetation composition dominated by hydrophytic plants. Some evidence of hydrophytic species decline and corresponding increase in upland plants, with upland species advancing from the riparian/upland interface.
2	Riparian site vegetation composition a roughly equal mix of hydrophytic and upland plant species. Upland species reproducing; little or no reproduction of hydrophytes. Water stress may be apparent in hydrophytic plants.
1	Riparian site vegetation composition dominated by upland species, with some extending to stream channel edge. Hydrophytic species mostly scattered clumps. In extreme cases, hydrophytic species may be totally lacking. Former aquifer presence may be indicated only by isolated hydrophytic remnants such as *Salix* stumps, etc.

3.33 Analysis of Riparian Condition Rating. Numerical rating values (1-4) have been assigned for each condition in the three attributes (Tables 1, 2, and 3).

A particular segment should be evaluated by systematically recording the condition of each attribute through an unbiased sampling scheme. The mean score provides a condition rating (Table 4). An example is provided.

Table 4. Riparian Condition Rating Values

Mean Rating Score	Rating
4	Excellent
3 - 3.9	Good
2 - 2.9	Fair
1 - 1.9	Poor

Example 1:

Attribute	Description	Rating
Streambank Soil Alteration	20% of bank is stable; 75% of bank is false.	
Vegetative Bank Protection	60% of bank covered; poor vigor; deep rooted plants greatly reduced	2
Aquifer Status Indicators	Upland plants 50-60%; hydrophytes declining; water stress apparent	2

Sum = 5
Mean = 5/3 = 1.7 (poor)

3.34 Considerations for use of the Riparian Condition Rating

(a) In considering inventory/management priority on a riparian site, at least six factors should be considered:

(1) Current riparian function and stability.

(2) Vulnerability of the site to future degradation, even though present condition may be good. Use of Pfankuch's (1975) stream reach inventory technique (or a modification outside USFS Region One) may be warranted. High management priority may be given to a "good condition-stable site," where the vulnerability to erosion is high.

(3) Channel dynamics, i.e., major channel adjustments vs. normal channel dynamics. Van Haveren and Jackson (1986) emphasize that "streams undergoing major adjustments should not be treated with habitat improvements until the channel has reached a new dynamic equilibrium."

(4) Causes of riparian site degradation due to both on-site and off-site (watershed) factors, must be understood.

(5) Potential for recovery, e.g., a stream in poor condition may have little potential for management response.

(6) Riparian dependent resource values.

(b) Other considerations include:

(1) Caution should be used in analyzing bare ground. The examiner should differentiate if this component is a result of natural floodplain deposition (bank building) or has resulted from overgrazing, trampling, trailing, or man's disturbance.

22

(2) If recent large-scale photography is available, field offices are encouraged to maximize the collection of data from this source for those parameters that can be identified. The riparian site condition rating and much of the extensive inventory may be completed through this means.

3.4 Supplemental Inventory Comments

Record any supplemental data available. The inventory field form (A) found in Appendix 2 includes headings for estimates of improvement potential, water source, man-made alterations, erosion processes, water quality impacts, and vegetation association and phase. Other factors may include grazing influences, wildlife use, watershed observations, ice conditions, indications of major hydrologic events and unique weather influences. Generally these observations require field analysis.

3.5 Riparian Dependent Resource Values

For values, enter none, low, moderate, or high (Form B, Appendix 2). For condition, enter N/A, poor, fair, good, or excellent. Comments may include anything pertinent to establishment of inventory or management priorities.

3.6 Vegetation Association and Phase

Where supplemental condition ratings are completed in the field, it may be possible to describe vegetation association and phase. This may be important if an intensive inventory will not be completed.

Vegetation association is based on the dominant species or set of species in both overstory and subordinate layers (Paysen et al., 1982). The association is a set of stable plant communities with a characteristic stand physiognomy and species composition in each of its layers.

Phase is a further refinement of association, using additional information (Paysen et al., 1982). Phase is identified based on percent aerial cover of trees, percent cover of herbaceous vegetation, presence of grazing impacts on the community, or age distribution of woody dominant species. In some cases, phase can be identified using aerial photography.

For purposes of classifying riparian vegetation, phases based on the following three plant community attributes can be recognized.

3.61 **Tree canopy cover.** For Riparian Forest Formations two Phases based on tree canopy cover can be recognized:

(a) **Forest**: 61% or greater tree canopy cover.

(b) **Woodland**: 26-60% tree canopy cover.

Tree canopy cover of 25% or less would place the community in a different phase. Where tree cover is 25% or less but is important to defining the character of a plant Association, this importance can be

23

reflected in the Association name. An example would be a *Salix lutea/ Glyceria striata* (*Populus tremuloides*) Association to describe a community with a sparse overstory of *Populus-tremuloides* (10-25% cover).

3.62 **Herbaceous cover.** Four phases based on the total (absolute) cover of herbs in the community can be recognized:

(a) 0-25% herb cover.

(b) 26-50% herb cover.

(c) 51-75% herb cover.

(d) 76% or greater herb cover

3.63 **Age distribution of woody dominant species.** The age distribution of the dominant trees and shrubs in the plant community can serve as an important indicator of change toward or away from the potential natural community. If, for example, a population of a dominant tree species exhibits only young age states (seedling to immature, vegetative), the species is invading the site and is often part of a seral community (Barbour et al., 1980). If, on the other hand, the tree species shows only older age states (from mature vegetative to senescence), it may not maintain itself in the community (Barbour et al., 1980). This can be either because it is part of a seral community and is being replaced by later seral species or because of perturbations that differentially impact the younger age states (e.g., livestock grazing, fire). Populations showing a mix of all age states, young to old, are likely part of the climax or potential natural community (Barbour et al., 1980). Figure 3 gives the possible combinations.

The following three phases attempt to display these important community characteristics. Because they apply to the dominant species the three Phases can only be used to modify Series or Association levels of classification. For example:

(a) **Young even-aged stand.** The dominant woody species is represented by a population composed of a disproportionate number of individuals in young age classes. Mature, reproductive individuals are rare or absent.

(b) **All-aged stand.** The dominant woody species is represented by a population made up of all age classes. In a forest community the number of mature, reproductive individuals may outnumber the young, immature individuals, but the latter are present in sufficient quantities to ensure adequate recruitment to sustain the population.

(c) **Old even-aged stand.** The dominant woody species is represented by a population comprised of a disproportionate number of individuals in old age classes. Seedlings and immature, vegetative individuals are rare or absent.

Other age distribution possibilities follow:

	Even	Mixed
Young-Aged	1	3
All-Aged		
Old-Aged	2	5

4. Intensive Riparian Ecological Site Inventory

4.1 General Considerations

4.11 Scope and Essential Components. Essential components of an intensive riparian ecological site inventory are listed in Tables 5 and 6. Optional inventory components maybe selected by the manager to reflect local needs and to help establishment of quantifiable management objectives (Table 7). The establishment of recommended minimum standards for inventory does not imply that previously collected data should be discarded. These data serve as valuable supplements and may be most responsive to local needs.

Table 5. Intensive Inventory - Essential Basin Components

Component	Method	References	Advantages	Disadvantages
a. Drainage pattern	USGS topo map	Chow (1964)	Quick and easy Little training required	Highly Subjective
b. Stream order analysis	USGS topo map	Chow (1964) Platts et al. (1983)	Little training required	Labor intensive
c. Elevation range	USGS topo map		No training required	

25

Table 6. Intensive Inventory - Essential Segment Components

Component	Method	References	Advantages	Disadvantages
a. Drainage area	Map planimeter		Automated planimeters available most BLM offices. Accurate to _0.01 mi.^{2} on 7 1/2 min. quads Little training required	Labor intensive
b. Latitude	USGS topo map		Easily obtained from maps	None
c. Orientation	USGS topo map			
d. Soil texture	Field measurement - Ribbon Method	USDA 1981 & 1983 w/trained specialist	Adequate accuracy specialists	Requires training
e. Soil Wetness	Field measurement - observe water table and/or mottling	USDA 1981 & 1983	Easily obtained in field	
f. Effective Soil Depth	Field measurement - depth measurement	USDA 1981 & 1983	Easily obtained in field	
g. Soil salinity	Field measurement - Observed plant type and growth - Meter	USDA 1981 & 1983	Easily obtained in field	
h. Soil Reaction	Field measurement - Colorimetric (pH Kit) - Electrometric (pH Meter)	USDA 1981 & 1983	Easily obtained in field	
i. Flooding	Photogrammetric and Field Evaluation	USDA 1981 & 1983	Obtained from Map (aerial photo interpretation)	
j. Susceptibility to Erosion	Interpretation of soil property data (K factor and Slope)	USDA 1981 & 1983	Easily obtained in field	
k. Channel Bankfull	Photogrammetric		Requires little training	Requires photo scale of 1:6,000 or larger. May require field verification. Requires some training to be able to identify bankfull features.
l. Channel Bankfull depth	Channel Geometry evaluation	Parsons and Hudson (1985)	Accuracy is good. Requires very little field work. Data analysis accomplished with an easy-to-use computer program.	Some training is required.

26

Table 6. Intensive Inventory - Essential Segment Components (continued)

Component	Method	References	Advantages	Disadvantages
m. Stream channel condition	Field assessment	Van Haveren and Jackson (1986)	Identifies stage of channel evolution and assesses recovery potential.	May require training for proper use.
n. Stream channel gradient	Map measurement		Quick and easy.	Requires 7-1/2 min or larger scale topo map. Accuracy is 4-10%.
	Field measure-Abney level		Quick field measurement Accuracy is _1%	None
	Field measure-Rod-and-level	Platts et al. (1983)	Accuracy is _0.01%	Cumbersome in the case of remote or heavily-vegetated streams.
o. Channel material	Ocular estimate	Pfankuch (1975)	Quick and easy	Precision not high.
p. Vegetation composition	Canopy cover	Daubenmire (1969) TR 4400-4 Canfield (1942)	Absolute data Efficient, Simple High precision (reproducible)	Large changes in canopy in response to climatic conditions.More difficult for tall trees.
q. SWA Area	Map measurement		Quick and easy.	Requires 7 1/2 min. or larger scale map or large scale photo. Requires more time.
	Pacing or measuring		Accuracy is good.	
r. Vegetation structure	Cover board	Nudds (1977)	Absolute data Good precision Index to many important riparian parameters. Simple.	Excludes cover above 2.5 meters. Carrying cover board cumbersome
	Canopy volume	Zamora (1981)	Absolute data Fair precision Index to many important riparian parameters. Simple. Three dimensional.	Excludes cover above 3.0 meters
	Canopy by height class		Simple Efficient Herbaceous & shrub components can be measured concurrently with canopy coverage composition.	Precision at tree height only fair. Only two dimensional.
	Spherical densitometer	Lemmon (1956, 1957) Hoffer (1962)	Simple. Efficient. Improves precision of "canopy by height" method for tall shrubs and trees.	Not applicable to herbaceous plants and most shrubs.

Table 7. Intensive Inventory - Optional Segment Components

Component	Method	References	Advantages	Disadvantages
a. Benthic Macro-Invertebrates	Surber Sampler	Surber (1936) Needham & Usinger (1956) Usinger (1956) Shannon and Weaver (1963) Wilhm (1972) Cooperrider et al. (1986, Chapter 32)	Easily used Data consistent with other studies Quantifiable area sampled. Rates fish food attributes	Not useable in deep water. Not useable in standing water. Some escape of organisms. Some organisms from outside sample areas collected. Requires large sample no's for numbers and biomass Influenced by off-site factors
b. Vegetation Species Frequency	Variable 4400-4	BLM Tech. Ref. types. Rapid	Applicable to all veg. Easily used Sensitive to change	Difficult to analyze
c. Woody Species Density	Quadrat	Strickler & Stearns (1962)	Quantifiable Simple Sensitive to changes in woody species	Individual plants sometimes difficult to identify Time consuming where woody sprouts abundant
d. Woody Species Form Classes	Form Class Assignment	Dasmann (1951) Cole (1958) Tech. Ref. 4400-3 Myers (1987)	Easily used Supplements other data with little effort	Requires training Vigor, age, and hedging has variable impacts on shrubs. Somewhat subjective Not absolute data
e. Woody Species Age Classes	Basal stem Diameter vs. Age	Myers (1987) Lonner (1972)	Key indicator of woody stand vigor Easily used Useful in describing veg. phases	Stem age may be less than oot age Factors other than age influenced diameter growth rates
f. Production	Weight Estimate	USDA (1976) BLM H-4410-1	Absolute data Best comparison of species. Useful for forage allocation	Labor intensive Human bias Significant training required. Difficult with shrubs and trees
g. Subsurface Water Level	Piezometer	Jackson et al. (1985)	Very precise Excellent monitoring tool	Requires careful handling and protection from stock. Requires training and careful design.

Pre-inventory planning must consider the possibility that riparian areas will be sampled intensively to develop adequate site descriptions for trend monitoring or for development of management of objectives. Where small and infrequent riparian site inclusions occur in an expansive livestock management pasture, management capability is typically low. Such small inclusions would probably be protected with fencing, where values justify it, and an intensive inventory would not be completed.

4.12 Potential Natural Community/Comparison Area. The potential natural community (PNC) of an ecological site is the "biotic community that could become established if all successional sequences were completed without interferences by man under the present environmental conditions" (Range Inventory and Standardization Committee 1983). The term "potential natural community" is preferred to the term "climax" to reflect realistically the conditions existing today (Range Inventory and Standardization Committee 1983). Since climax presumes a self replicating community, riparian PNC are not climax (i.e., cottonwoods).

Classification allows the selection of a "comparison area" (CA) of the same association/phase, which has the same, or similar, potential. The CA may be representative of the PNC where examples are available, or it may represent an ecologically advanced association which meets the various resource value objectives. It should be the intent of field offices to systematically collect and store riparian vegetation and physical site data on as many comparison areas as possible, so that classification and resource value ratings may be modified to reflect local or regional potential (Crouse and Kindschy, 1981). Construction of exclosures representative of a variety of riparian associations will facilitate this process. Private lands should not be overlooked as sources of CAs.

PNC is not a precise assembly of species for which the proportions are the same from place to place, or even in the same place from year to year. Variability, within reasonable limits is the rule rather than the exception (USDA, 1976). Riparian ecological site descriptions should represent several CA's that are differentiated on the basis of similar site characteristics. An ecological site description should ultimately be prepared for each site type.

The Bureau goal should be to document and characterize riparian associations within various seral stages. This will enhance the manager's capability to develop objectives based upon predicted riparian site response. A seral stage which provides for soil and water conservation may meet a preferred resource objective better than PNC in some cases.

4.13 Riparian Ecological Site Delineation. Delineation of riparian ecological sites often is complicated by the apparent lack of discreet boundaries as one proceeds up or down a drainage (Dick-Peddie and Hubbard, 1977). Norton et al. (1981) observed a tendency for different riparian communities to appear as mosaics within a riparian zone. This "clumping effect" is usually defined on a micro-site basis, or it may represent changes in channel meander, rather than in the physical character of the site.

Site delineation will be aided by considering broad geographic definitions (Crouse and Kindschy, 1981). **Significant differences in site characteristics and in the kinds and proportions of dominant plant species are the main criteria for differentiating riparian ecological sites.**

Identification of the aquatic/riparian and riparian/upland interfaces along the moisture gradient (profile) is difficult, since by definition, the riparian ecosystem is transitional between aquatic and terrestrial ecosystems. This often narrow riparian site is juxtaposed between an aquatic site containing only hydrophytic species and an upland site in which all species are intolerant to prolonged saturated soil conditions within the root zone during the growing season (Hart, 1984).

Delineation of the riparian/upland interface requires experienced judgement, in considering both the physical character of the site and significant vegetation composition change. In using "indicator species" to define this interface it must be recognized that species presence and absence is also influenced by factors other than moisture, e.g., disturbance, grazing, pathogens, weather extremes, competitive interactions, and random variations (Hart, 1984). Delineation may be further complicated by degradation of the physical structure of the riparian site.

The riparian ecological site along streams coincides broadly with Pfankuch's (1975) definition for upper streambank as the area between the normal high water line and the next break in the general slope of the surrounding land (Figure 9). Platts et al. (1983) defined the riparian ecosystem as including the streambank and the floodplain, and as the vegetation portion of the streamside environment. This definition would then exclude the unvegetated lower bank area.

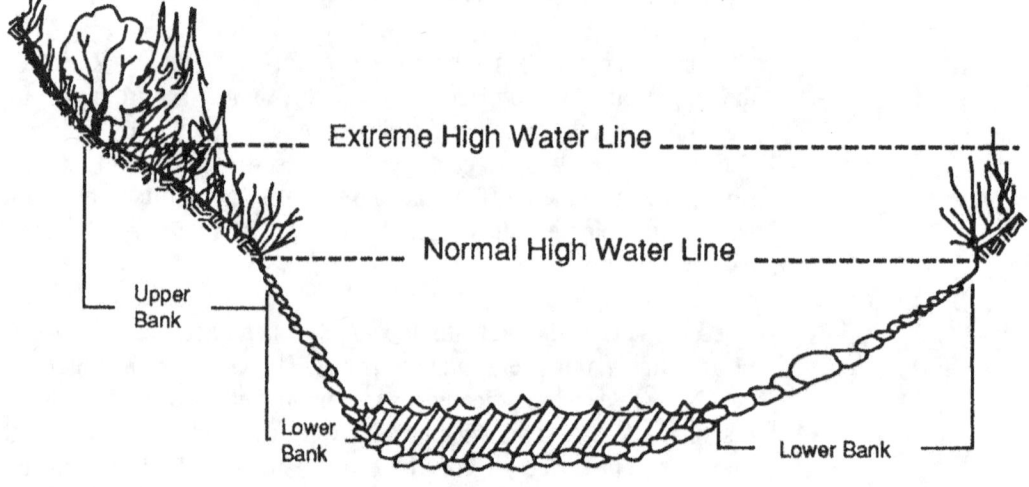

Figure 9. Upper streambank area from Pfankuch (1975).

4.14   **Timing and Frequency.** Inventories should preferably be timed to facilitate adequate vegetation species identification and quantification. Ideally, peak of flowering is desired for species identification.

4.2   **Procedures for Essential Inventory Components**

4.21   **Site Writeup Area.** The SWA should be the smallest delineated area where vegetation data are collected. SWA's can be delineated as predominately a single site with or without inclusions of small areas of other sites, or as a complex of two or more sites so interspersed as to be impracticable to separate for the contemplated management of the area.

The analysis of aerial photography, combined with geographic interpretations on USGS quadrangle maps in the extensive inventory should provide tentative SWA boundaries based on physical site character and vegetation series. Fences, pasture boundaries, and allotment boundaries must be located on photos and/or maps. SWAs should not extend beyond a fenced management pasture, allotment, or other administrative boundary. More than one SWA may occur within a pasture, however, if the site character changes. SWAs represent different seral stages of an ecological site.

On small streams, the SWA will generally include both sides. Where there are site differences, each side should comprise a separate SWA, especially where the stream is large enough to be a livestock barrier.

On small-scale photography, field mapping may consist of delineating a stream length without concern for mapping riparian area width. SWA boundary adjustment will be made in the field on the basis of site differences not detected in the extensive inventory. Two approaches to SWA mapping are considered:

(1) SWA and riparian site boundaries are synonymous where there are no inclusions of other sites or seral stages are not involved.

(2) The SWA boundary may include more than one riparian site or seral stage of the same site. In these situations, each of the vegetation communities are described but not separately mapped. An estimate of the percentage area of each vegetation unit within the SWA is recorded on the site writeup documents.

4.22   Segment Components (Field Form C, Appendix 2)

(a) **Soil Mapping.** Where detailed soil surveys have been made, field observations may not be necessary. However, where order 3 soil surveys were not detailed enough to map out riparian areas, field observations will be needed at selected sites to determine key soil properties. Most riparian areas are mapped as complexes, associations, and undifferentiated map units because of the intricate and complex occurrence of soils within these areas. These map units will generally provide an adequate intensive soil inventory.

(b) **Soil Texture with Rock Fragment Modifier and Stoniness Class.** Where the fine distinctions in textural classes are needed and available, they would be used. However, due to the variability of soils that commonly occur within riparian areas (mixed alluvial soils), a general broad group of textural classes can be effectively used. An outline of acceptable general terms in three classes and in five classes in relation to the basic soil textural classes names is shown in 3.22 (f). Adjectives used as texture class names where rock fragment occur are:

(1) no term for volumes of rock fragments less than 15 percent;

31

(2) gravelly, cobbly, stoney, or bouldery for volumes of 15 to 30 percent;

(3) very gravelly, very cobbly, very stoney or very bouldery for volumes of 30 to 60 percent; and

(4) extremely for volumes greater than 60 percent.

(c) **Soil Wetness.** The degrees and patterns of wetness are described. Phases are used to differentiate among classes of soil water states, water table levels, and soil drainage where the ranges of such properties within a soil taxon are needed. Phases related to soil wetness are (1) drained: (including excessively drained, well drained and moderately well drained), and (2) somewhat poorly drained and poorly drained (including very poorly drained). Altered drainage is used where changes have occurred in the natural soil water condition. Such changes are commonly due to a deepening of the stream channel or to the filling of depressions or to wetness due to seepage from drainages or irrigation systems.

Soils that have a seasonal high water table are classified according to depth to the water table, kind of water table, and time of year when the water table is highest.

Depth. The normal depth range of a seasonal high water table or zone of saturation of the natural undrained soil is given to the nearest half-foot. The highest water level is given first, e.g., 1.5-3.0. Water above the surface is shown by a positive whole number, e.g., +3-1.5. A symbol of 6.0 means that the water table is below 6 feet or that a water table exists for less than a few weeks.

Kind. Three kinds of seasonal high water tables are recognized within the soil: apparent, perched, and artesian. A fourth kind, ponding, is above the soil surface.

(1) **Apparent water table** is the level at which water stands in a freshly dug, unlined borehole after adequate time for adjust ments in the surrounding soil.

(2) **Perched water table** is one that exists in the soil above an unsaturated zone. A water table may be inferred to be perched on the basis of general knowledge of the water levels of an area, the landscape position, the permeability of soil layers, and from other evidence. To prove that a water table is perched, the water levels in boreholes must be observed to fall when the borehole is extended.

(3) **Artesian water table** is one that exists under hydrostatic head beneath an impermeable layer, when the impermeable layer has been penetrated by a case borehole, the water rises. The final level of the water in the cased borehole may then be character ized as an artesian water table.

(4) **Ponding** is water above the soil surface.

Season (Months). The period when the water table normally persists at the average highest depth is recorded in months, for example, December - April.

(d) **Soil Effective Rooting Depth.** The depth of soil material that plant roots can penetrate readily to obtain water and plant nutrients. Depth is expressed as shallow (1-20 in. [2.5-7.8 cm]), moderately deep (20-40 in. [7.8-15.7 cm]), and deep (40 in. [15.7] or greater).

(e) **Soil Salinity.** Salinity phases are used to distinguish between degrees of salinity within the range of a soil series or taxon of a higher category. The observed plant type and growth are evidence for recognizing salinity. Electrical conductivity values can be used as a guide. Degrees of salinity are: 1) slightly saline, 2) moderately saline, and 3) strongly saline (USDA, 1983).

(f) **Soil Reaction.** Soil alkalinity or acidity is an important property affecting plant composition, plant growth, soil use, and management. The degree of alkalinity in a soil is expressed by pH values and associated terminology. Refer to Soil Survey Manual (USDA, 1981) for degrees of reaction.

(g) **Soil Erosion Susceptibility.** This is a measure of the susceptibility of a soil to erosion when the surface is exposed (no cover present). It is based on infiltration rate, movement of water, and water storage. Classes of erosion susceptibility are slight, moderate, and high (USDA, 1981).

(h) **Flooding.** Flooding is the temporary covering of the soil surface by flowing water from any source, such as streams overflowing their banks, runoff from adjacent or surrounding slopes, or any combination of these sources. Flooding classes are expressed by frequency, duration, and time of year:

(1) **Frequency Classes.**

None — No reasonable possibility of flooding (near 0 percent chance of flooding in any year).

Rare — Flooding unlikely but possible under unusual weather conditions (from near 0 to 5 percent chance of flooding in any year, or 0 to 5 times in 100 years).

Occasional — Flooding is expected infrequently under usual weather conditions (5 to 50 percent chance of flooding in any year, or 5 to 50 times in 100 years).

Frequent -- Flooding is likely to occur often under usual weather conditions (more than 50 percent chance of flooding in any year, or more than 50 times in 100 years).

Common -- Occasional and frequent classes can be grouped forcertain purposes and called **common** flooding.

(2) **Duration Classes.** Average duration of inundation per flood occurrence is given only for occasional and frequent classes.

Very Brief — less than 2 days.

Brief — 2 to less than 7 days.

Long — 7 days to 1 month.

Very Long — more than 1 month.

(3) **Season.** The time of year when floods are likely to occur isexpressed in months, for example, February - April. The time period expressed should include 2/3 to 3/4 of the occurrences. Time and duration of the flood are the most critical factors determining the growth and survival of a given plan species.

(i) **Channel Bankfull Width.** The average width of the stream channel at bankfull stage (refer to Figure 9).

(j) **Channel Bankfull Depth.** The average depth of the stream channel at bankfull flow (refer to Figure 10). Depth should be measured along a tape 1/4, 1/2, and 3/4 the distance across the stream. The sum of these three measurements divided by four equals average depth.

(k) **Width/Depth Ratio.** Bankfull width divided by depth is the width/depth ratio. It is a useful parameter for monitoring and classifying streams because it expresses the relationship between channel geometry, discharge, potential, and preferred channel size.

(l) **Stream Channel Condition.** The geomorphic and hydrologic stability, in terms of channel morphologic parameters, of a given stream reach as described by Van Haveren and Jackson (1986). For incised channels, refer to Forms A through E (Figure 11). For channels with lateral erosion, refer to Forms X, Y, or Z (Figure 12).

(m) **Stream Channel Gradient.** Gradient was estimated from quadrangle maps in the extensive inventory to provide a mean figure for the SWA. This should be refined in the field by using an abney or level to characterize gradient of the channel. Measurement can be along the wetted edge or in the thalweg, and from pool to pool or from riffle to riffle.

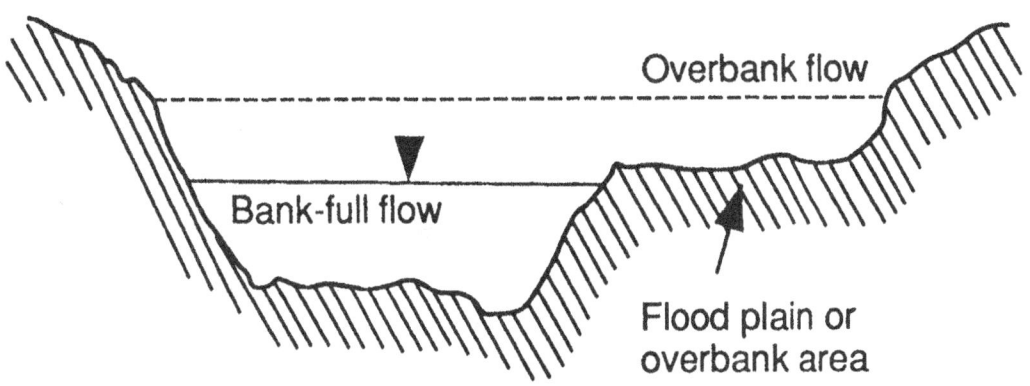

Figure 10. Stream channel cross-section showing approximate stages for bankfull and overbank flows.

(n) **Dominant Channel Material.** Schumm (1977) and Bray (1982) discuss the significance of bank and bed material in determining the overall shape of the channel. Record channel materials using criteria from Pfankuch (1975), with the total composition equalling 100%:

  (1) Exposed bedrock
  (2) Large boulders 3 ft. + diameter
  (3) Small boulders 1-3 ft. diameter
  (4) Large rubble 6-12 in.
  (5) Small rubble, 3-6 in.
  (6) Coarse gravel 1-3 in.
  (7) Fine gravel 0.1-1 in.
  (8) Sand, silt, clay, muck

(o) **Vegetation Composition.** The vegetation inventory will be of the present community species composition as measured by canopy coverage. Composition is the proportion or relative abundance of species in the community. Species composition is a primary means of describing successional stages and seral communities. It reflects the status of a species relative to the total community. Composition is an interpretive item derived from absolute data.

Canopy cover (Field Form D, Appendix 2) is the recommended minimum attribute of vegetation to be collected for determination of species composition. The weight estimate method is an option to canopy coverage. Composition by either weight or canopy cover is used in conjunction with riparian site descriptions to determine the degree of similarity between the present vegetation association and the potential natural community. Additional vegetation attributes may be measured as necessary for management.

The same method (canopy or weight) must be used for analyzing the present community and for developing riparian site descriptions. **Composition computed from weight is not comparable to that computed from canopy coverage.**

35

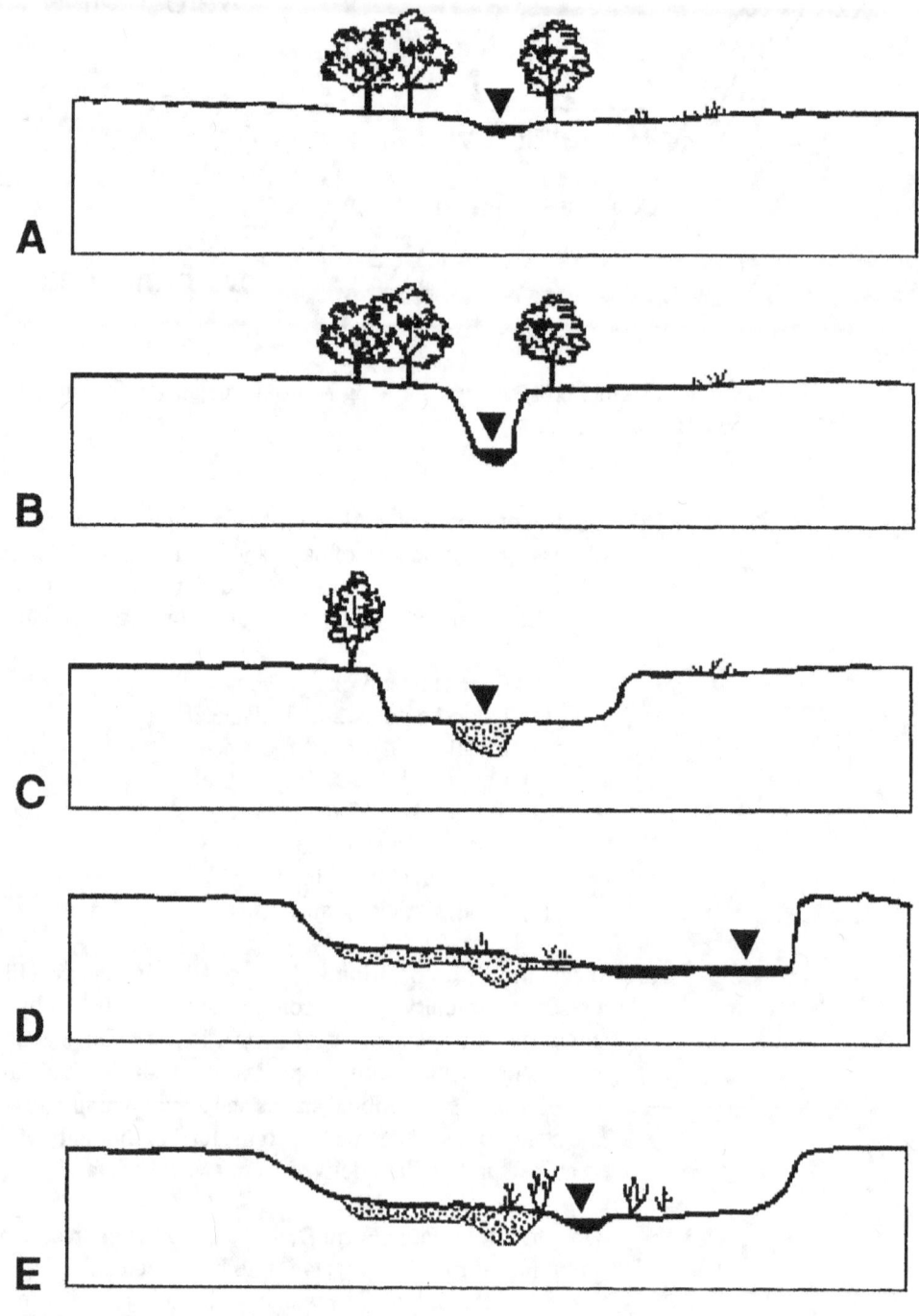

Figure 11. Hypothetical sequence of arroyo evolution from Van Haveren and Jackson (1986).

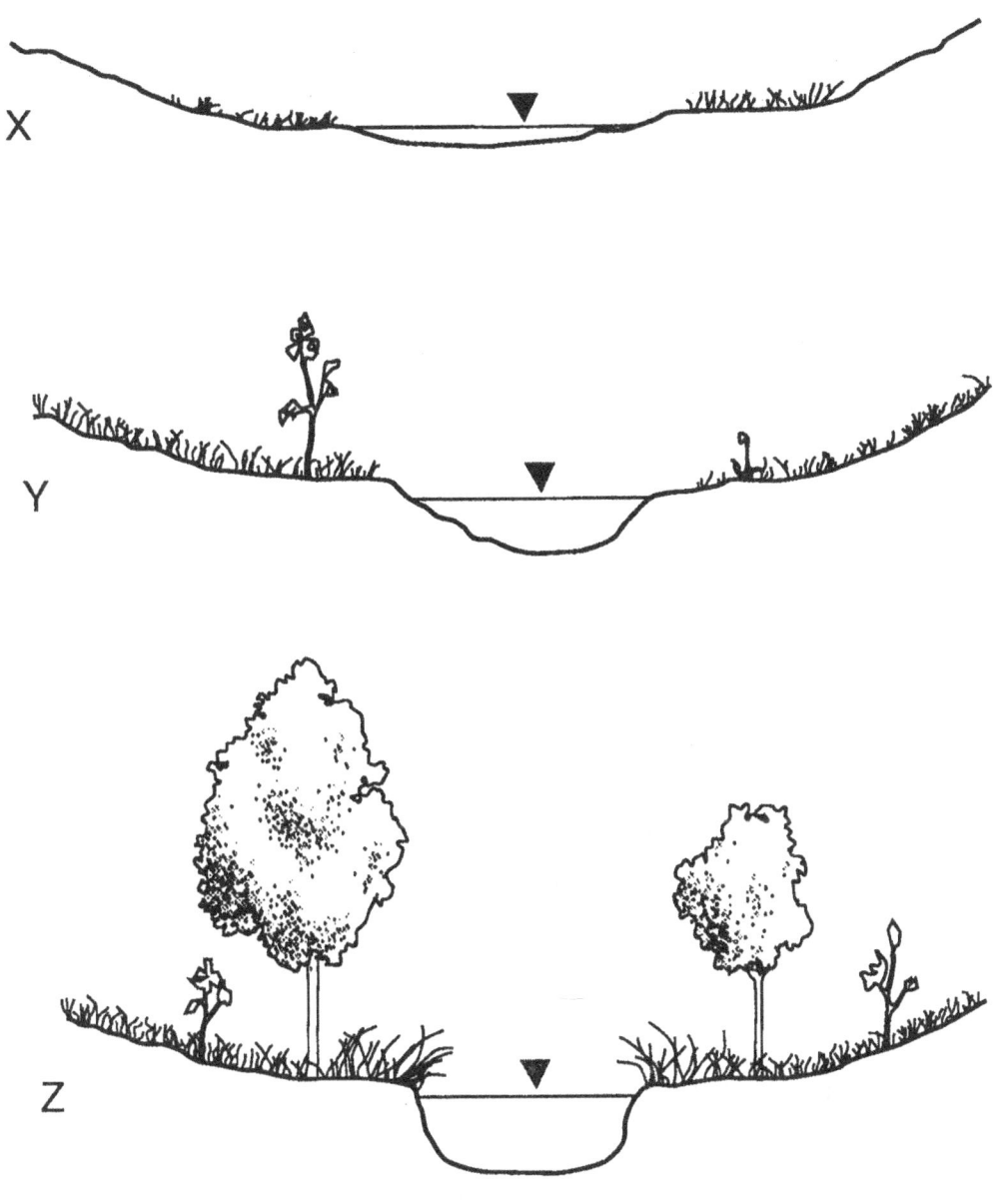

Figure 12. Hypothetical sequence of non-incised stream channel evolution from laterally unstable (x) to laterally stable condition (z) from Van Haveren and Jackson (1986).

Canopy cover measurements include small openings in the canopy, and consequently yield a higher percentage figure than basal cover or foliar cover. It provides a relative index of species ecological dominance. Total canopy cover of all species in the community may exceed 100% because overlapping plant canopies are common. Species composition is the canopy coverage of the species in question divided by the canopy coverage of all species. A modification of the Daubenmire (1959) canopy coverage classes is recommended (Table 8). Normally a minimum of 40 plots should be read on a SWA.

(p) **Site Writeup Area.** The dimensions of the SWA (segment) provide information for assessing wildlife habitat value, stocking rate compilations, floodplain functions, and for planning purposes. If measurements (as opposed to estimates) are used, it may also be a trend indicator.

SWA length will generally be derived from a 1:24,000 quadrangle map or large-scale aerial photograph, using a map-measuring tool. Where resource values are high, or objectives warrant, SWA length may be paced or measured. SWA width should be paced or measured each time a composition quadrat is measured, since average riparian site width has trend value. Several sites could be permanently monumented, if desired, to monitor trend in riparian site width. Section 4.13 (site delineation) should be reviewed.

(q) **Riparian Vegetation Structure.** Vegetation structure is a general term which relates to the spatial function of vegetation. It is broadly alluded to by wildlife biologists in use of the term "cover." Vegetation structure is implied in data compiled by growth form (herbaceous, shrub, tree).

Table 8. Recommended Canopy Cover Classes for Measuring Vegetation Composition Modified from Daubenmire (1959).

Cover Class	Range of Coverage(%)	Midpoint(%)
0	0	0.0
T	<1	0.5
1	1 - 5	3.5
2	5 - 25	15.0
3	25 - 50	37.5
4	50 - 75	62.5
5	75 - 95	85.0
6	95 - 100	97.5

Structure reflects and influences many important riparian site characters, functions, and values, such as grazing, wildlife cover, successional stage, vegetation vigor, thermoregulation, sediment filtering-bank building, site stability-vulnerability, energy cycle and

38

many others. Riparian sites with diverse vegetation structures will generally have higher resource values. Structure data will help establish quantifiable resource management objectives.

Four techniques are described for estimating vegetation structure although many others have been developed (Lyon, 1968; Bently et al., 1970; Peek, 1970; Neiman, 1977; Bryant and Kothman, 1979). Two of the described methods, "Vegetation Profile Board" and Shrub Canopy Volume, have the disadvantage of not including tree cover over 10 ft. tall in their original form.

(1) **Canopy Coverage by Height Category.** This is the simplest and most practical alternative. It consists of recording the canopy coverage data for composition by height category (Field Form F, Appendix 2). The most simple categories for analysis are herbaceous, shrub, and tree. Data could also be recorded by species, if required for management objectives.

Height categories, if used, should be dictated by structure and management objectives. Examples of categories are: 0-0.25 ft. (0-0.08 m), 0.25-2 ft. (0.08-0.6 m), 2-5 ft. (0.6-1.5m), 5-10 ft.; (1.5-3 m), 10-25 ft. (3-8 m), 25+ ft. (8+ m).

(2) **Vegetation Profile Board** (Field Form G, Appendix 2). A "vegetation profile board" (Figure 13) has been successfully used to identify variations in the vegetation structure (height classes) of habitats utilized by rodents (M'Closkey and Field-wick, 1975) and birds (MacArthur and MacArthur, 1961, and Recher, 1981).

A modification of the profile board was developed for use in white-tailed deer habitat by Nudds (1977). The board is 8.25 ft. (2.5 m) high, 12 in. (30.48 cm) wide and is cut from a 3/8-in. (1.90- cm) plywood.

It is marked in black and white alternating colors, at 19.7- in. (0.5- m) intervals (Figure 13). Two aluminum spikes are attached to the bottom of the board so that it can be held upright in the ground. This feature allows one person to collect data. The spikes are removable so that a hinged support arm can be used to hold the board upright on frozen ground. The board weighs about 7.5 lbs. (3.4 kg) and is maneuverable in most vegetation. The board could be lengthened to 3 or 4 meters, if desired, but this would necessitate hinging it in the middle to facilitate handling.

The standard observing distance was determined to be 50 ft. (15 m); the distance which gave the greatest variation to assure discrimination among microhabitats (Gysel and Lyon 1980). This distance can be modified using techniques described by Nudds (1977).

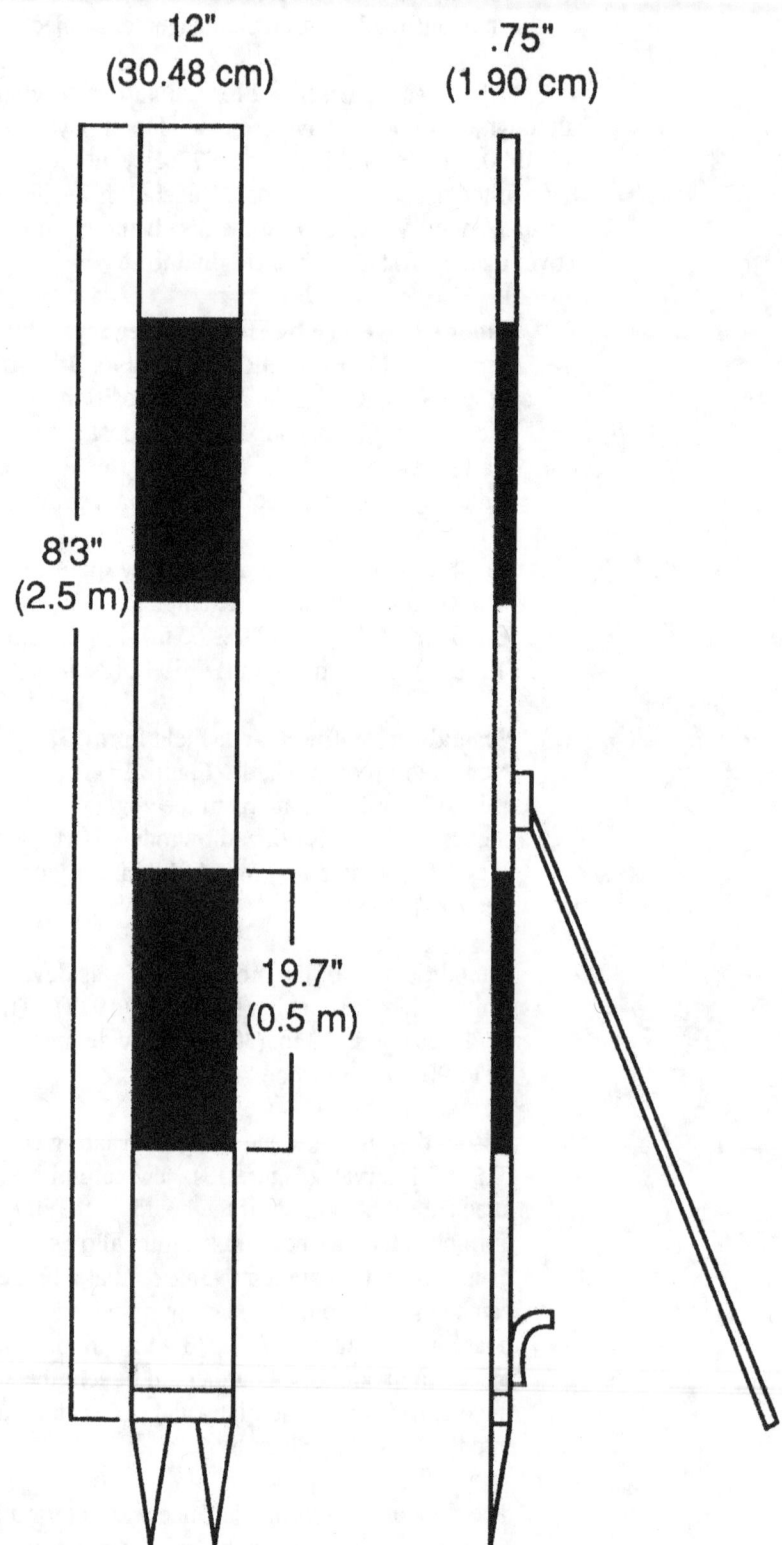

Figure 13. Vegetation profile board from Nudds (1977).

The board is used in the following manner to estimate vertical cover at five height intervals. The board is set in the ground and read at a distance of 15 m (50 ft.) in a randomly chosen direction from a randomly selected point in each habitat to be measured. The proportion of each 18- in. interval (vertical quadrate) covered by vegetation is estimated and tallied. Data can be recorded by using a single-digit "density score" from 1 to 5 that corresponds to the mean value of a range of quintiles (e.g., 1 corresponds to a range of 0 to 20%, 2 to a range of 21 to 40%, etc.) (Nudds, 1977). It is suggested that in BLM inventories the modified Daubenmire criteria (Table 8) for canopy coverage can be used to simplify field work and analysis.

Cover data may be recorded as one consolidated entry, by growth form (grass, forb, shrub, etc.) or by species, depending upon management objectives. As in the measure of canopy coverage, overlap may result in total cover values in excess of 100%.

At least two cover board readings should be taken at each plot site extending 15 m (50 ft.) up and down the transect line. If riparian site width allows, two additional samples should be taken at 90° angles to the transect.

Once the data are collected, foliage profiles can be graphically constructed (Figure 14). These profiles then allow an analysis of temporal changes in the vegetation structure within habitats. They can also be used to compare habitats and determine differences among habitats usually considered similar because of their vegetation classification. The use of this board and the vegetation profiles can be used to monitor changes over time in important habitat by using permanently marked points so that the cover board can be photographed (Myers 1987).

(3) **Shrub Canopy Volume.** Data from the "Shrub Canopy Volume" technique can be used to determine and compare dominance of plant species in plant communities (Daubenmire, 1968). The method described in this section was patterned by Zamora (1981) after procedures developed by Daubenmire (1959) for measuring canopy coverage. It requires a three-dimensional plot 1 m2 with a 3-meter vertical dimension (Figure 15). The plot size and shape can be modified according to the nature of the vegetation being sampled. The plot can be located by any sampling technique. The plot boundaries are delineated by using three poles, 1 meter long, marked in decimeters. Although Zamora (1981) adapted the technique for measurement of shrubs, any vegetation structure could be analyzed.

Within the boundaries of each plot, total canopy volume is estimated for each shrub species and recorded as one of eight volume classes. Each estimate includes the canopy of a species

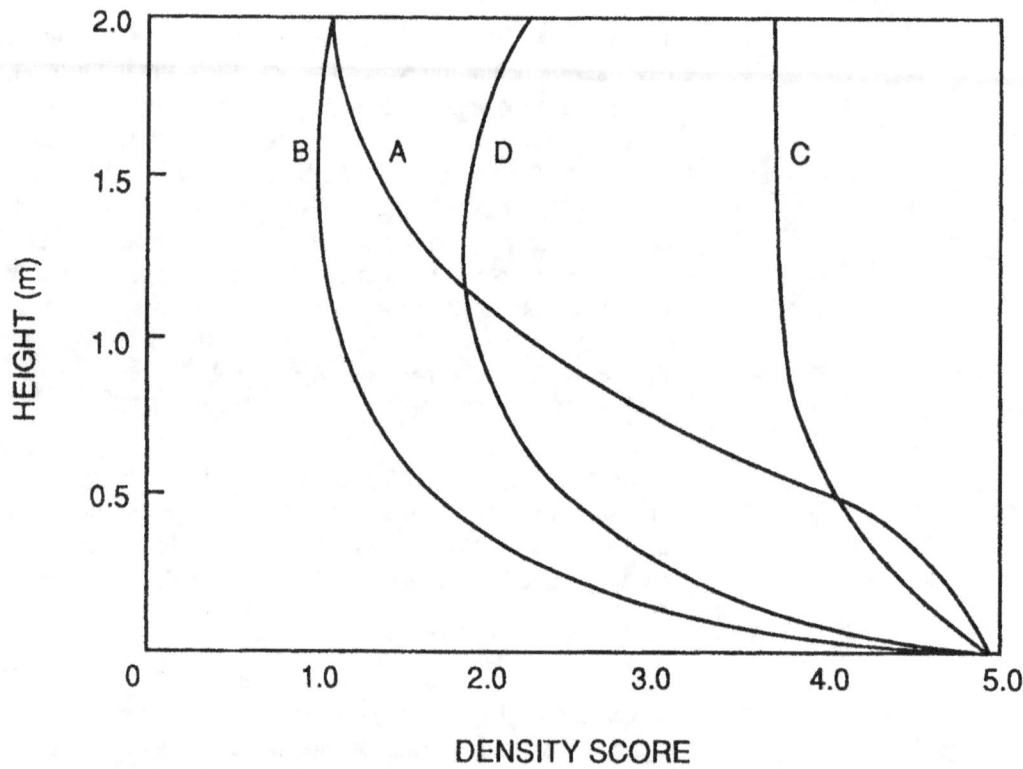

Figure 14. Foliage profiles for four vegetation types from Nudds (1977).

growing inside the plot and also overhanging canopies of species growing outside the plot. Where the canopies of two or more species are intertwined, the canopies are estimated separately. The vegetation canopy volume at different strata could be estimated at any desired intervals. Examples might be: 0 - 1/2 m; 1/2 - 1 m; 1 - 1-1/2 m; 1-1/2 - 2 m; 2 - 3 m. As in the cover board technique, vegetation canopy volume may be consolidated, recorded by growth form, or by species, depending upon management objectives. Canopy volume estimate for a plot may exceed 100 percent.

This technique could be modified to include canopy volume estimates of trees and shrubs up to 4 m high.

For descriptions of volume classes, dimensions used to estimate the upper limits of volume classes, and guidance on sample sizes, refer to Zamora (1981).

(4) **Point Intercept-Spherical Densitometer.** The densitometer can be used to estimate the canopy cover of very tall shrubs and trees. It would serve as a supplement to the "Canopy Coverage by Height Method." All canopy coverage estimates and densitometer measurements should be recorded by appropriate height categories for tall species.

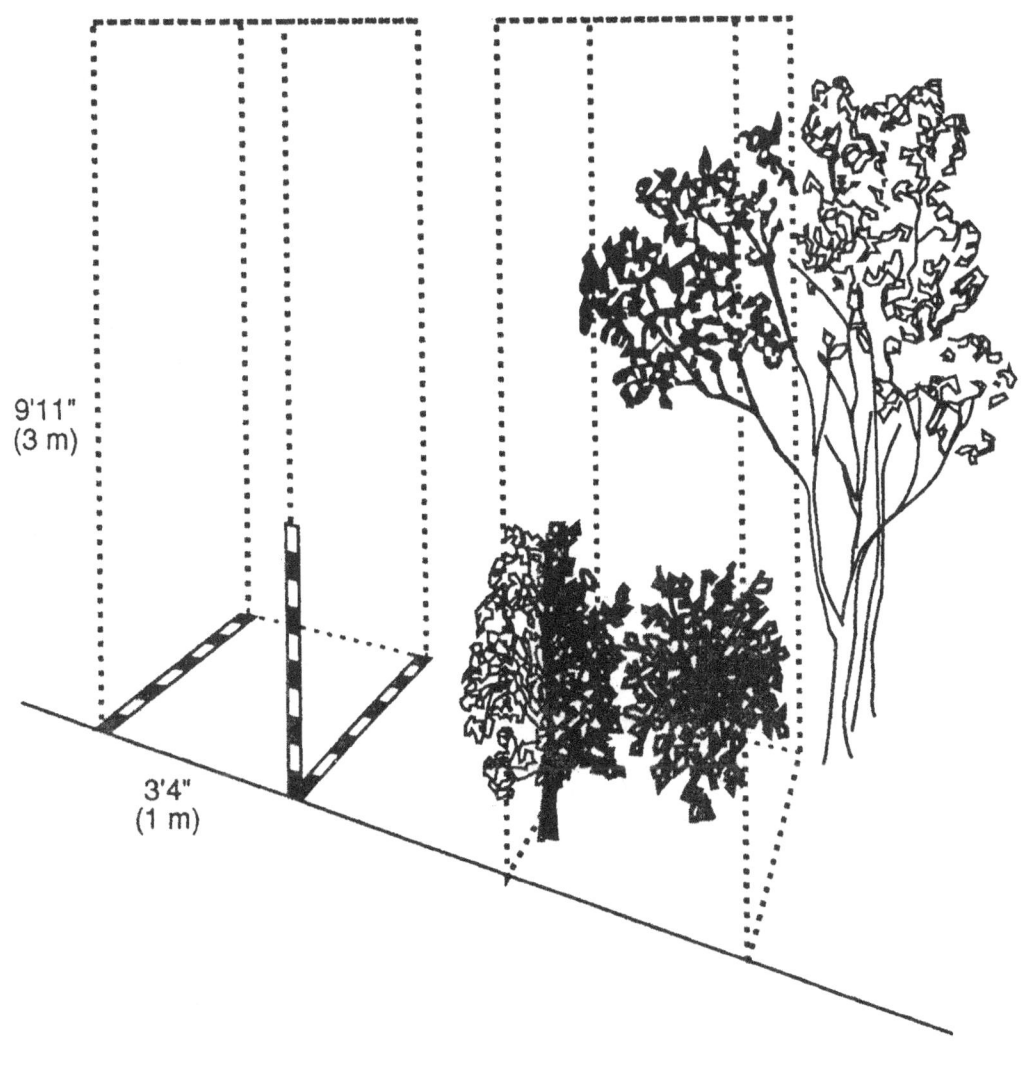

9'11"
(3 m)

3'4"
(1 m)

Figure 15. Canopy volume plot from Zamora (1981). Only that porion of a canopy that falls within the plot is used in making the volume estimates as illustrated by the darkly shaded areas.

In practice, random sampling locations are selected and at each of these locations the person using the densitometer looks at each of the points on the meter and records sky or the kind of plant which is intercepted. If the point hits plant parts from more than one species, all should be recorded as hits. For estimates of canopy cover, the operator must judge where the outer perimeter of the canopies of individual plants lie, and then record for each sample point whether or not it falls within a plant's perimeter. The only data that need to be recorded are the total number of points intercepting each category of interest (e.g., trees or tall shrubs by species and sky). At each sample location, data are collected by observing in four directions (north, east, south, and west).

To calculate cover for a particular category of data (i.e., plant species x), the following equation is used:

$$C_x = \frac{n_x}{n}\ (100)$$

where C_x = cover of x(%)

n_x = number of dots intercepting x

n = total number of dots sampled

This formula may be applied for either foliar or canopy cover, depending upon how the data were collected. Commercially available densiometers use a 96-dot grid. Approximate measures of cover may be made by assuming each dot equals 1% (on the average). This will give an error of less than 5% due to the difference between 96 and 100.

Lemmon (1956) reported that the spherical densitometer consistently produces accurate measurements regardless of the operator, but did not provide data to support the statement. Densitometer measurements were found to be highly correlated with those taken with a canopy camera (Hoffer 1962).

This technique can be used by one person and is particularly appropriate to use where vegetation is dense and cover estimates by species are desirable.

The instructions accompanying the instrument are adequate; however, field experience is necessary to improve operator consistency. Usually 15 minutes instruction and one-half hour practice is adequate.

(r) **Transect Systems for Canopy Coverage.** Extensive inventory data are used in designing transects before initiating fieldwork. The manager must design the transect for the SWA based upon:

(1) desired precision for sampling dominant plants;

(2) variability of vegetation;

(3) size of plants; and

(4) riparian site width.

Any recognized technique for measuring canopy coverage may be used (USDI, 1985a). Where tall, woody vegetation occurs, some techniques may be impractical. Two optional techniques are described below. They are designed to minimize bias in woody vegetation associations, while allowing flexibility in transect design.

(1) **Riparian Site Transect with Nested Quadrats.** Divide SWA length by the number of required transects plus one so as not to sample on the SWA boundary. Divide again by the step length of the surveyor. This is the step interval between transect lines. If 20 samples are required, with only one quadrat on each transect, step interval is determined by dividing SWA length by 21 (20 transects plus 1). Where 20 samples are desired, with two quadrats per transect, step interval is SWA length divided by 11 (10 transects plus 1).

Stepping should be initiated from a relocatable site or monument, e.g., fence, section corner, reference post, or tributary confluence. Both beginning and ending points should be further referenced with photographs taken in at least two directions from the starting point, e.g., upstream and downstream.

If desired, a portion of the transects and quadrats can be permanently monumented with rebar for trend purposes (see section 5.32).

When the transect line is located from stepping, a flag or lath should mark it. This establishes the point at which a transect line is established perpendicular to the stream. After recording the width of the riparian site and transect line, a table of random numbers is used for selecting the number of steps to the sample point(s) along the transect line.

Where riparian sites are exceptionally narrow, only one quadrat can be located on a transect (Figure 16). On wide riparian sites, numerous quadrats should be located on each transect to adequately sample the association, and transects will routinely alternate between sides of the stream (Figure 17).

Quadrats may be rectangular to conform to the linear shape of the riverine riparian site, with the long axis parallel to the stream (Figure 16). Quadrats may be of various sizes for the herbaceous, shrub, and tree components, as dictated by plant

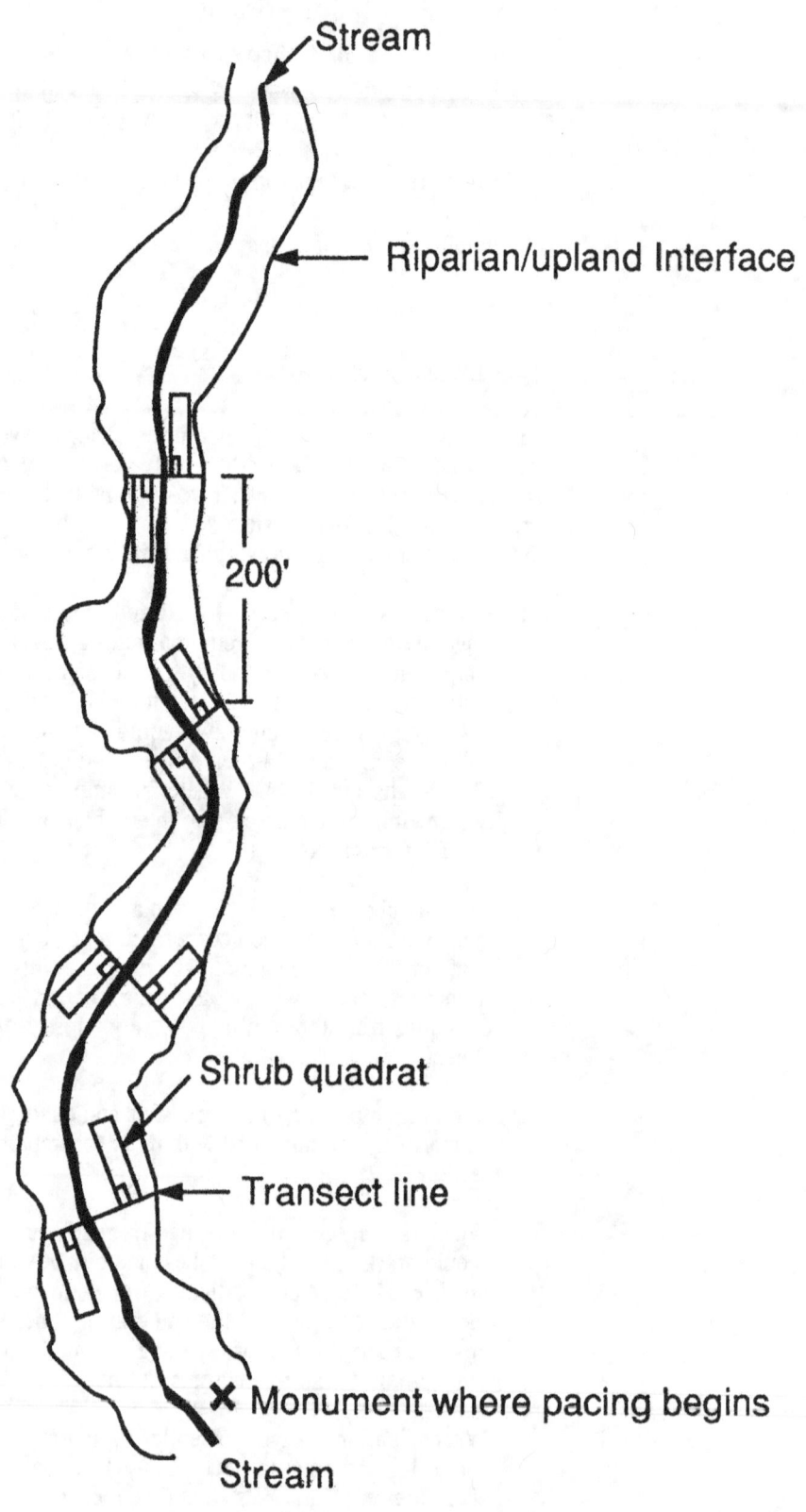

Figure 16. Transect layout on an exceptionally narrow riverine SWA, with only one large shrub quadrat on each side of the stream, and 200' (74 steps) between transect lines. Smaller quadrats are nested within the corner nearest the sample point.

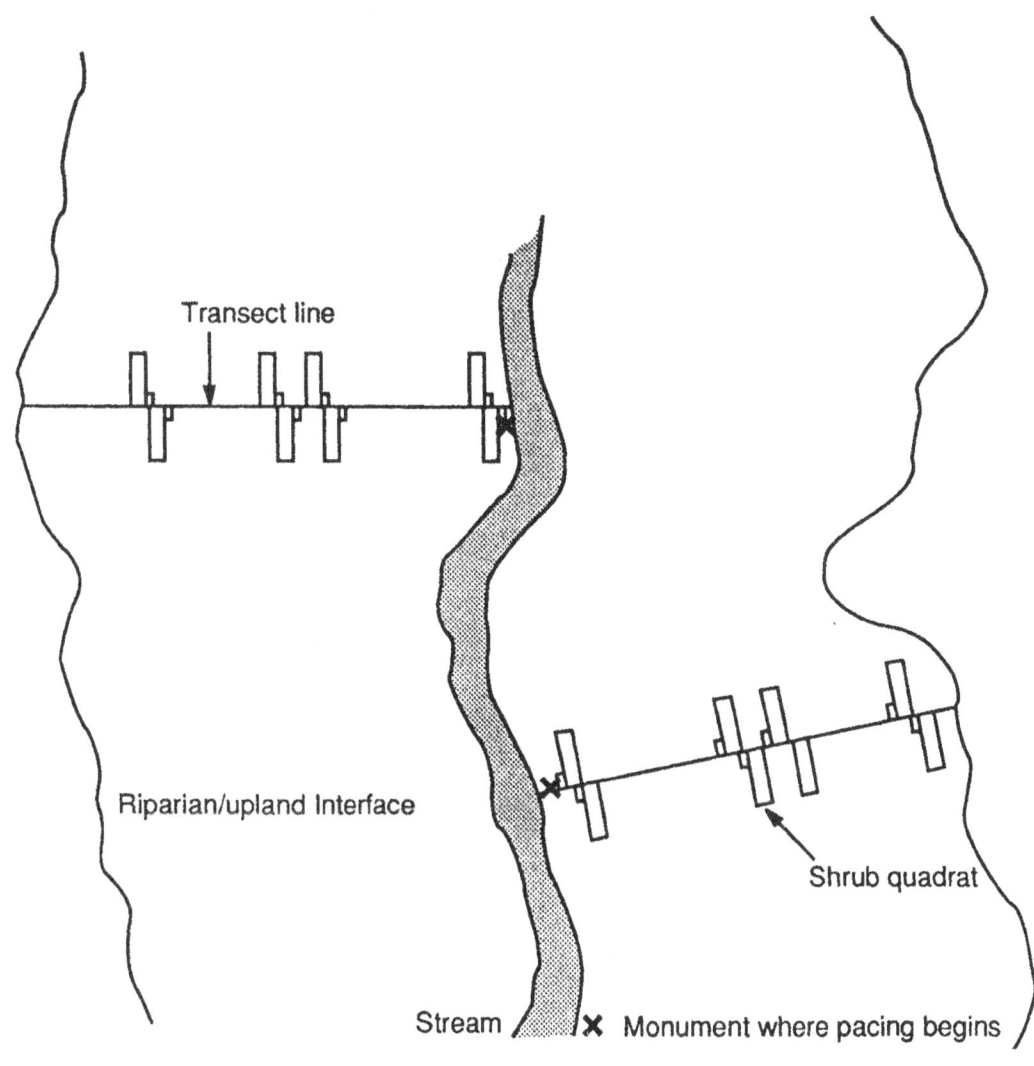

Transect line

Riparian/upland Interface

Shrub quadrat

Stream   X Monument where pacing begins

Figure 17.   Transect layout on a wide riverine SWA, with eight large shrub quadrats on each transect line. Smaller quadrats for herbaceous species are nested within the corner nearest the sample point. Quadrat locations on the transects are established by using a table of random numbers.

size and sampling efficiency (Table 9). Trees are those species exceeding 6 meters (20 feet) when mature. Quadrat size must remain consistent through the course of an inventory. Smaller quadrats are "nested" within the corner of the larger quadrate which is nearest the sampling point.

Table 9. Examples of Plot Sizes for Canopy Coverage Measurements

Component	Dimensions	Area (m²)
Herbaceous	2 x 5 dcm	0.1
	Variable	1.0
Shrub	1 x 2 m	2
	2 x 4 m	8
	2 x 8 m	16
	4 x 8 m	32
Tree	4 x 8 m	32
	4 x 16 m	64
	4 x 25 m	100

If a quadrat is selected for an unsuitable site as a result of meander or other factors, or includes stream channel or predominantly upland vegetation another random number should be selected.

(2) **Daubenmire Nested Quadrat.** Daubenmire (1968) identified a nested quadrat technique to incorporate analysis of shrubs and trees. Selection of quadrat layout sites may follow the criteria described previously, or any technique that minimizes bias.

This method employs the use of 1 to 3 adjoining quadrats measuring 5 x 20 meters, with smaller, 20- x 50-cm or 40- x 50-cm quadrats nested inside (Figure 18). The small quadrats measure herbaceous canopy, one large quadrat measures shrub canopy, and two or three quadrats measure tree canopy. Where trees are lacking, one 5- x 20-meter quadrat suffices, making this technique suitable to use in narrow riparian sites.

4.3   Procedures for Selective Optional Intensive Inventory Components

4.31   Segment Components. Optional components are selected as needed to reflect management objectives. (Table 7)

(a) **Benthic Macroinvertebrates.** Benthic macroinvertebrate composition is an indirect measure of riverine riparian vegetation condition through its influence on the aquatic environment. It can be a valuable supplement to the inventory data base and a trend indicator. Four critical influences in which invertebrate monitoring may be especially sensitive include (1) sediment load, (2) temperature, (3) instream flow, and (4) nutrient loading.

Resource managers must recognize that factors other than on-site riparian vegetation influence macroinvertebrate composition, e.g.,

48

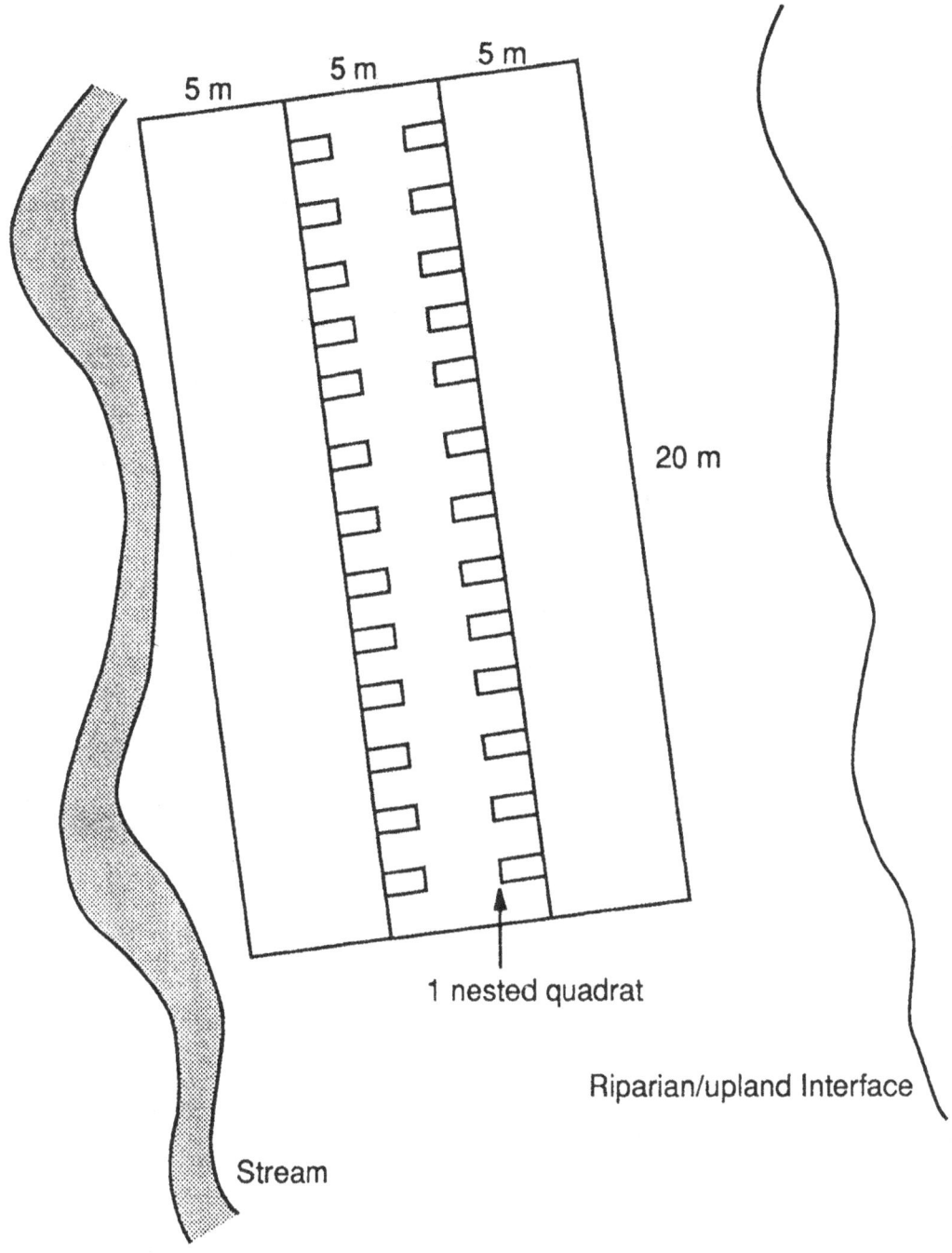

Figure 18. Nested quadrat technique from Daubenmire (1968). The small nested quadrats (20 x 50 x 40 x 50 cm) measure herbaceous canopy. One 5- x 20-m quadrat measures shrub canopy and two or three are used for measuring tree canopy.

upstream watershed influences, water quantity-quality, major hydrologic events, and beaver activity. Season also has a major influence on benthic composition due to species differences in seasonal emergence.

Two levels of environmental parameters are involved in describing what organisms may be found in a stream. The first is macro-scale parameters such as, riparian vegetation, aspect, elevation, zoogeography, climatic and hydrochemical conditions (Usinger, 1956). Most of these parameters have been analyzed in the intensive inventory. The second set of interrelated parameters are important in determining microdistribution. They include substrate, current velocity, and distribution of food particles (Cummins, 1962). The distribution of substrate type controls the diversity of microhabitat. A diverse substrate leads to a greater diversity among the fauna.

The Surber sampler (Surber, 1936) is preferred for sampling because it is simple and widely used, thus data collected with it will be comparable to most other studies.
For data analysis, refer to Chapter 32 of Inventory and Monitoring of Wildlife Habitat (Cooperrider et al., 1986).

(b) **Vegetation Species Frequency.** Frequency is the probability of encountering a species within a series of uniformly sized plots. Generally the species must be rooted within the quadrat. However, some procedures allow frequency tallies for overhanging canopies of woody vegetation. Frequency data are directly related to the size of the sampling frame or plot; as plot size increases, frequency increases. One size of frame is not appropriate for all species. The nested frequency concept utilizes a nested plot configuration to acquire adequate data on a greater number of species. BLM Technical References 4400-4 and 4400-7 discuss frequency techniques and concepts.

(c) **Woody Species Density.** Density is the number of individuals per unit of area or its reciprocal as mean area per individual. Density is particularly applicable to analyses of tree and shrub populations. It is a sensitive measure of trend, particularly for young age classes, and a valuable supplement where management objectives relate to woody regeneration.

Quadrats used for canopy measurements of shrubs and trees are used for density measurements. Count by species all plants rooted within the quadrat. Identification of individual plants may be difficult at times. An individual rooted plant stem or shoot is often considered as the counting unit (Strickler and Stearns, 1962). Where density of woody regeneration is a management objective, quadrats should be permanently monumented for monitoring purposes. Density measurements are time-consuming where woody sprouts are abundant.

(d) **Woody Species Form, Vigor, and Utilization Classes.** Utilization and vigor criteria for shrubs and small trees are described in TR 4400-3.

Form classes found useful in Montana riparian surveys (Myers, 1987) are:

(1) **Unavailable** - plants provide no forage or herbage below 1.5 meters in height.

(2) **Normal** - plants have fewer then 50% of the available second year and older leaders clipped and are neither decadent or dead.

(3) **Heavily Hedged** - plants have 50% or more of the available second year (not current annual growth) or older leaders clipped, and are not dead. Do not consider leaders above 1.5 meters high. If all leaders are unavailable, the plant cannot be heavily hedged. Hedging can be identified as attributable to livestock, big game, beaver, etc., when practical or desired.

(4) **Decadent** - plants have 30% or more of the canopy area dead. A decadent plant meeting the heavily hedged criteria is recorded as hedged.

(5) **Hedged Dead** - plants have no living tissue where mortality is clearly attributable to heavy hedging.

(6) **Dead** - plants have no living tissue.

(e) **Woody Species Age Classes.** Age distribution of dominant shrub and tree species is an important indicator of stand vigor. In analyzing grazing impacts in Montana, Myers (1981) noted that excessive "hot season" use reduced regeneration of **Salix spp.,** changing age-class structure to the point where old plants dominated, resulting in eventual losses of willow species in the composition (Figure 19). Myers (1981) further showed that on ungrazed areas and well-managed grazing allotments, young-age (1-4 years) willows exceeded dead and decadent willows.

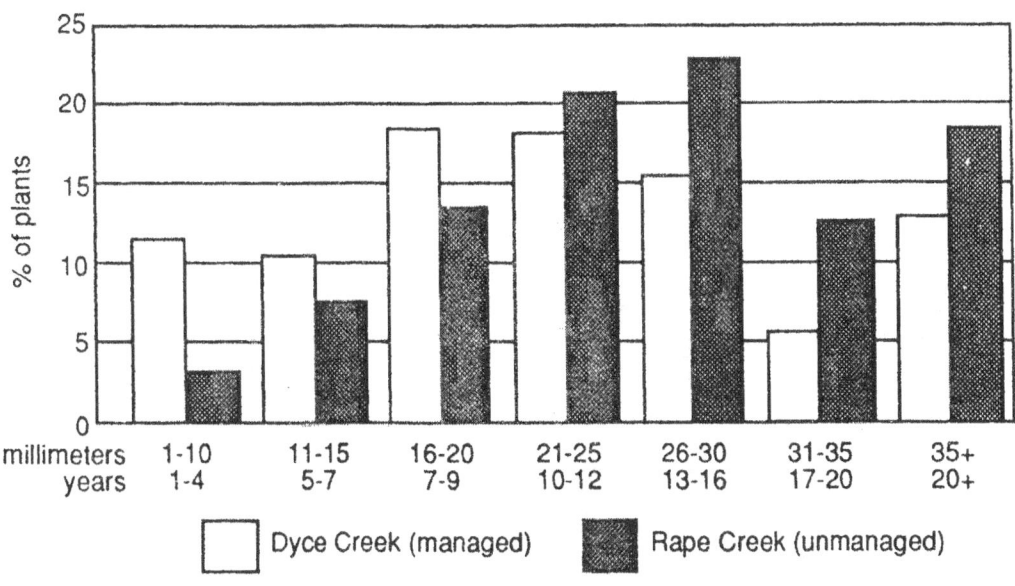

Figure 19. Distribution of willow size-age classes on an unmanaged stream and a well-managed stream (Myers 1987).

51

In evaluating age-class characteristics of riparian shrubs in Montana, Myers (1987) established valid correlations between basal stem diameter (BSD) and age on light- to moderately-grazed willows, aspen, water birch, and other species (Table 10). Mean basal diameter of the largest live stem on a plant was measured and compared to stem age as indicated by growth-ring counts. Correlation coefficient (r) values were all valid at the 99% level. The 95% confidence

Table 10. Basal Stem Diameter/Age Relationship for Three Woody Riparian Species in Montana [1]

Age	N	Basal Stem Diameter Mean (mm)	C.I. (95%)	Correlation Coefficient (r)
Salix boothii and S. geyeriana				
2	6	7.83	±1.32	
3	17	8.94	±1.14	
4	13	8.61	±2.02	
5	10	12.6	±2.59	
6	8	13.62	±4.53	
7	11	13.81	±4.97	
8	9	19.00	±8.15	
9	11	18.27	±4.67	
0	4	17.25	±7.41	
11	2	24.00	±4.24	
	91			r = 0.9503
Populus tremuloides				
5	8	9.63	±2.60	
6	7	13.28	±2.87	
7	6	13.80	±2.85	
8	5	20.60	±11.08	
9	3	22.00	±3.00	
10	4	22.25	±6.40	
11	2	24.00	±4.25	
	35			r = 0.9576
Betula occidentalis				
4	8	9.62	±3.29	
5	5	13.40	±3.36	
6	6	11.33	±2.65	
7	2	16.00	±2.82	
8	3	14.00	±6.24	
9	2	17.00	±7.07	
11	4	19.50	±8.42	
12	3	18.66	±4.04	
19	2	52.50	±34.64	
	35			r = 0.9242

[1] *From Myers (1987)*

52

intervals for mean BSDs showed that most plants (willow, aspen, birch) under 10 mm were about 4 years of age or less. Three size-age categories 1-10 mm, 11-15 mm, and +15 mm were successfully used in analyzing age-class characteristics of woody species in riparian associations with emphasis on regeneration.

Size-age criteria should be established through size-age analysis to reflect local environmental influences on growth. There is little information on woody species growth patterns as they relate to diameter. Most work with aspen considers the influence of site on plant height (Jones, 1967; Baker, 1925). Aspen diameter growth is not related to site the same way that height growth is; the site characteristics that limited heights did not limit relative diameter growth (Jones and Schier, 1985). It has been recognized, however, that insects, competition, dominance, climate and old age influence diameter growth rates.

Comparisons of the ages of roots and stems from multi- stemmed maple and serviceberry in Montana showed that the largest root ranged from 10 to 36 years older than the largest stems (Lonner 1972). For practical reasons, BLM field efforts should recognize this limitation in using "stem age" for age-class analysis.

Lonner (1972) found significant correlations between age and root crown stem area and between age and stem cross- section diameter in 11 Montana shrubs, including two species sometimes found in riparian sites, Rocky Mountain maple (*Acer glabrum*) and choke-cherry (*Prunus virginiana*). Lonner suggested maximum stem diameter could have practical application for field use in estimating age of browse species having a single main stem.

Age classes for shrubs, as described by Dasmann (1951) and as modified by Cole (1958), are very crude indicators of age, and are not recommended in riparian inventories. These age classes, widely used in some browse studies, defined seedlings, young, and mature plants as stem base one-eighth inch or less, one-eighth to one-fourth inch, and stem base over one-fourth inch, respectively (BLM Technical Reference 4400-3).

Relative indices of "stem age," sufficient for management purposes can be developed for riparian site shrubs using growth ring-basal stem diameter correlations (Table 10). On larger deciduous trees, the same criteria might be used with "diameter at breast height" (DBH) measurements and increment bore analysis for aging.

In interpreting woody age-class data, a predominance of young age-classes may be indicative of a seral community (Barbour et al., 1980) or prevailing environmental conditions, such as flooding, which sustain a seral stage. If only older plants occur, the species may be declining as a result of succession or because of mortality of regeneration from grazing, or other factors.

Section 3.6 describes vegetation phases based on age distribution of woody species. Where woody regeneration is a management concern these phases are very descriptive.

(f) **Vegetatio Production.** Production and its use in calculating composition is ecologically sound, but labor-intensive. The Production data are collected on a weight basis, through estimation or a combination of estimation and harvesting (double sampling) (USDI, 1976 and 1981). Where small inclusions or micro-sites add irregularity to vegetative distribution, more intensive sampling (20 plots) may be required (USDA, 1976 [Section 6043]). Normally, 10 plots will be read on a SWA.

(g) **Subsurface Water Level.** A knowledge of subsurface water level may be critical to interpretation of vegetation data, and it has value as a monitoring tool. In the extensive inventory (3.32c), subsurface water status was evaluated indirectly through its influence on hydrophytic plants. Installation of small-diameter observation wells (piezometers) is a more precise method and is relatively easy. Sampling and statistical design must be carefully considered (Jackson et al., 1985). A brief review of groundwater measurement techniques is provided by Gilliland (1969).

Experience with piezometers in the Prineville, Oregon, BLM district in riparian sites resulted in following recommendations (Elmore, 1987):

(1) Use 1-1/2 inch PVC

(2) Drill holes in the lower 2/3 of the pipe.

(3) Space series of holes one inch apart vertically, with four holes in each series spaced equally around the pipe circumference.

(4) Cover the pipe with fabric (polyester worked well).

(5) A cap, with an airhole, must be placed on the pipe in such a fashion that it can be easily removed without displacing or moving the pipe.

(6) The PVC pipe was buried with the use of a tree planter, by excavating a 2 inch hole.

(7) Water level observations were recorded with the use of a well logger, which is a small light built to allow the water surface to complete a circuit.

4.4 Other Sources of Inventory Methodology

(a) Methods for Evaluating Riparian Habitats with Applications to Management (Platts et al, 1987).

(b) Stream Channel Cross Section Surveys and Data Analysis (Parsons and Hudson, 1985).

(c) Integrated Riparian Evaluation Guide - Draft (USDA, FS, Intermountain Region, 1988).

(d) Riparian Inventory and Monitoring (Myers, 1987).

5. Monitoring

5.1 General Considerations

5.11 Monitoring Objectives. Monitoring is the process by which progress toward meeting management objectives is measured. The monitoring of riparian areas will involve varying degrees of intensity and complexity depending on the ecological site and the priority placed upon its management. In all cases the specific monitoring components must be selected based on the objectives found in the land-use or activity plan. BLM Technical References 4400-1, Planning for Monitoring, and 4400-7, Analysis, Interpretation and Evaluation, discuss objectives and the criteria used to establish and modify resource objectives.

5.12 Monitoring Intensity. There are two levels of intensity for riparian area monitoring: Level I Monitoring includes areas producing their potential, are not deteriorated, or produce few resource benefits. Level II Monitoring includes riparian areas which have a high potential to improve, produce multiple-use benefits, and are currently in a deteriorated state.

Level I Monitoring, as a minimum, consists of permanently monumented photographic documentation or aerial photography supplemented with narrative descriptions of observations taken over a period of time. Simple documentation of observed changes in woody vegetation along stream courses may be sufficient for many low-priority management areas. The vegetation profile board technique (Section 4.23 q) is well suited to this. If a decline in resource condition is observed Level I Monitoring serves as the rationale for implementing the more intense Level II Monitoring.

All documentation must attempt an explanation of the cause- and-effect relationship that may be occurring. For example, if a 100-year flood has scoured stream banks and deposited sediments throughout the riparian area, there is every reason to expect a change in the vegetation component. Livestock grazing impacts may be obvious; however, the relationship between beaver and livestock grazing may require more thought, i.e., as beaver use stimulates woody sprouting, livestock impacts may become more critical. Level II areas generally receive intense monitoring scrutiny. As a minimum, it is recommended these areas be monitored for changes in canopy cover, species composition, structure, and woody species density. Sampling may include collecting woody species data by age and form class. Photographic documentation may include aspect photography with a wide-angle lens and/or using the vegetation profile board technique (Section 4.23 s). Other attributes of vegetation may be sampled as management objectives dictate.

5.13 Frequency and Timing of Monitoring. The frequency and timing of monitoring should be dependent upon four factors:

(1) the management objectives and time frames for achieving them;

(2) the minimum period of time in which one can expect to detect change;

(3) the times when change in management is scheduled or possible (e.g., renewal of a grazing lease); and

(4)   the grazing system cycle; duplication of studies should coincide with the same grazing treatments.

In general, few situations will require measurements more frequently than once a year (except for techniques such as utilization that require before and after measurements in one year). Monitoring should be done at least every 5 years.

5.14   **Minimum Monitoring Standards.** States and Districts should develop minimum monitoring standards appropriate for the local riparian types and communities and the local management problems and objectives. The standards should reflect the minimum amount of information required to determine if management objectives are or are not being achieved. A suggested minimum standard for the Bureau will be photography adequate to determine change in structure of the plant community, e.g., change from a forb-grass-dominated to a low-shrub, high-shrub or tree community, or vice-versa. This may be done with either large-scale (1:1,000-4,000) low level aerial photography or with ground photography from monumented photo-plots. Under most circumstances additional measurements will be required.

5.2   **The Monitoring Plan.** The Resource Area or District monitoring plan should be completed prior to establishing riparian monitoring studies. The plan should describe how riparian site measurements will be taken and how data will be used to determine if management objectives are being met. Specifics, e.g., maps and transect data, should be in the activity plan.

At a minimum, the Resource Area or District plan should address the following topics:

I.   Introduction

      Provide a general overview of the monitoring plan, i.e., purpose for monitoring, participating or cooperating agencies, and how multidisciplinary input will be coordinated.

II.   Objective(s)

      Emphasize the importance of developing management objectives that are concise, measurable, and explicit. Describe how monitoring techniques relate to management objectives.

III. Limiting Factors and/or Critical Riparian Components

      Emphasize the need to narrow down the limiting or critical riparian components to be measured. Measure only those components that are critical to the management decisions stated in the objectives. Define minimum standards for monitoring for Level I and Level II areas.

IV.   Monitoring Techniques

      Describe resource components to be monitored and list the techniques that will be used for each component. Describe all techniques, criteria, and definitions in sufficient detail to assure continuity in future use. Clearly state all assumptions and known limitations for the use of each technique. Provide forms for recording data.

56

V.   Frequency and Duration

Describe requirements for time of year, conditions, etc. when measurements should be taken and the interval between measurements.

VI.   Data Analysis, Interpretation, Evaluation and Presentation

Describe how the data collected will be analyzed, who will interpret and
evaluate it, and how and to whom it will be presented. Provide forms for
analyzing data.

VII.   Decision Threshold Levels

Describe appropriate decision threshold levels, i.e., measurable riparian
conditions that indicate whether or not management objectives are being
achieved, and that will be used to change management if necessary.

5.3   Procedures for Monitoring

5.31   Physical Components (Abiotic). The key to any effective riparian
monitoring strategy is the careful identification of those processes of
interest and the development of a sampling design and data analysis that
will quantify the effects of management actions.

Measurements of riparian physical features must relate either directly or
indirectly to the established riparian management objectives. Direct
monitoring includes the measurement of the physical process or variable
to be influenced by the management action. Indirect monitoring is the
measurement of an indicator variable and an inference of the relationship
of that indicator variable to the physical process or resource variable of
direct interest to management.

In alluvial or other self-adjusting stream channels, channel physical
features, including width, depth, cross-sectional area, wetted perimeter,
channel gradient, sinuosity, and bed material size, all vary with local
hydrologic, geologic, and vegetation conditions. In other words, every
stream channel assumes a unique set of morphological characteristics in
response to its past and present watershed condition.

In self-forming channels (channels not controlled by bedrock), channel
geometry variables can be monitored over time using permanent cross-
section locations (Parsons and Hudson, 1985). One application of this
procedure would be the documentation of stream channel recovery from
an unstable regime to a more stable condition (Van Haveren and Jackson,
1986).

Stream channel stability ratings (Pfankuch, 1975), although somewhat
subjective in application, may be used to monitor geomorphic stability of
a channel over time. When used outside of USFS Region One, some
attributes need to be adjusted.

Hydrologic variables of interest in riparian management include peak or
design discharge rates, seasonal low-flow discharge rates, water-table
elevations, and sediment transport over time or through a given site.
Water-quality variables of interest include water temperature, turbidity,
dissolved oxygen, and total dissolved solids. Water-quality variables
should never be included in a monitoring program without concurrent

measurements of stream discharge at the same sampling location. Ponce (1981) provides excellent guidance on water-quality monitoring and Williams and Thomas (1984) offer guidelines on collection and analysis of sediment data in wildland situations.

Subsurface water levels (of depth to the water table) are important to the establishment and maintenance of riparian vegetation. Piezometers are discussed in Sec. 4.31(g).

Since hydrologic processes can change rapidly in time or space in response to both natural and man-caused events, monitoring of hydrologic variables is a complex undertaking. Particular attention must be given to choice of sampling location, sample size, and statistical design. Desired degrees of accuracy and precision must be determined before deciding on a monitoring strategy.

5.32 **Vegetation Components (Biotic).** A riparian area monitoring program may involve one or more of the following attributes of vegetation, as determined by management objectives:

> Density
> Frequency
> Cover
>> basal
>> foliar
>> canopy
>> ground
> Production
> Structure
> Species composition (derived from cover or production)
> Dead crown, decadence
> Form classes
> Age classes (or size-age classes)
> Diameter at breast height (DBH)
> Plant height

The monitoring program may sample any of the above by age or form class. For example, cottonwood density could be sampled by the number mature per acre, the number decadent per acre, the number of saplings per acre and the number of seedlings per acre. The same holds true for cover, frequency, etc. Technical Reference 4400-7, Analysis, Interpretation, and Evaluation defines and discusses most of the attributes of vegetation. These attributes are also discussed in the Intensive Inventory section (4.2, 4.3) of this reference document. Inventories may be duplicated all or in part, so long as permanent monuments are established initially.

5.33 **Other Components (Resources).** Biotic components other than vegetation may be monitored. This may include indirect monitoring of macroinvertebrates, breeding birds or fishes. Components such as macroinvertebrates are very sensitive indicators of changes in conditions such as water quality (Section 4.31a). Bird or fish surveys may be directly related to management objectives of fish production or bird diversity. For guidance on such techniques, refer to "Inventory and Monitoring of Wildlife Habitat" (Cooperrider et al., 1986).

5.34 Resource Uses

(a) **Grazing.** Grazing utilization of riparian areas by wild and domestic animals can have a significant influence on the relative health of vegetation. Utilization techniques must be designed to provide data on acceptable and unacceptable use levels, frequency of use, duration of use, and season of use. Technical References 4400-3 and TR1737-4 discuss utilization techniques and philosophies. Utilization should include consideration of woody as well as herbaceous species.

Utilization data collected during the growing season may have varying value as pertaining to influence on riparian site function, due to regrowth. It may be required to monitor impacts on other uses, e.g, wildlife cover. The physical impacts of livestock, e.g., trampling damage and rubbing damage may be more significant than utilization during the growing season. Utilization data relate more to riparian site physical function (stability, sediment entrapment, insulation, shading, etc.) if collected after the growing season.

(b) **Recreation Use.** Recreationists make intensive use of riparian areas and can cause deterioration of the riparian site, particularly soils and vegetation.

Soils. The two key impacts are compaction and removal. The observable type of activities that will cause these impacts are human and vehicular movement. Repeated human and vehicle use applied over a period of time will compact the soil, contributing to the reduction of moisture infiltration and increasing overland flow and erosion. Persons seeking quality topsoil may also remove soil from riparian sites.

Vegetation. The key impacts on the vegetation are trampling, cutting, and removal. Woody species are often used for firewood and cooking sticks. Shrubs and flowering species are vulnerable to removal. All species are impacted adversely by soil compaction.

Developed recreation facilities will create greater impacts to the riparian values because of the concentration of human and vehicular use. Facilities that intensify use are parking areas, spurs and roads, camp and picnic sites, restrooms, hydrants, grills, tables, and tent sites.

Dispersed recreation will generally not contribute to excessive impact; however, high levels of use can create impacts of the same magnitude as those in developed facilities. Areas which should be monitored include fishing sites, trails, off-road vehicle use areas, vehicular stream crossings, and viewing or interpretive sites.

Management objectives for recreation use should consider impacts on riparian sites. The limits of acceptable change created by recreation use should be established by monitoring soils and vegetation characteristics. Techniques will not differ from those used in monitoring livestock or wildlife impacts.

5.4 Developing a Monitoring System

5.41 Relating Monitoring to Management Objectives. The process of relating monitoring to management objectives should include the following steps:

(a) Identify riparian ecological site (BLM Handbook H-4410-1).

(b) Determine current ecological status.

(c) Characterize resource values for various successional stages of the site.

(d) Select the desired successional stage (desired plant community).

(e) Develop resource value ratings (RVR's) for the desired plant community which reflect management objectives.

(f) Monitor the RVR's.

5.42 Ecological Status. Ecological status (BLM Handbook H-4410-1, Sec. 305) is based on comparison of the existing plant community with that of the PNC. Where PNCs or successionally advanced comparison areas are not described, ecological status is difficult to establish.

Ecological status is not synonymous with riparian management condition. Riparian management condition is based on resource management objectives, of which ecological status is one consideration. Management for a desired seral stage (desired plant community) may be a prerequisite to meeting the objectives for the site.

The existing community maybe compared with the PNC or CA using a similarity index $\frac{2W}{a+b}$ where "a" is the sum of the species values for the measured attribute "b" is the sum of values in the PNC and "W" is the sum of the values common to both.

Absolute (e.g., canopy coverage) or relative (e.g., percent composition) data can be used; however, the resulting values will differ somewhat. The same formula should be used to analyze both absolute and relative data, and the mean figure used to derive the coefficient of community similarity.

The coefficient of community similarity represents a degree of mathematical similarity or overlap between the existing community and a PNC. It is important to recognize that two communities with the same mathematical similarity coefficient, and the same potential, may be very dissimilar in composition. This is because their similarities (overlap) with the PNC may be based upon different portions of the PNC composition. Four classes (USDI, 1981) are used to express the degree to which the composition of the present community reflects that of the PNC.

Ecological Status	Percent of Present Plant Community that is PNC
PNC	76 - 100
Late seral	51 - 75
Mid seral	26 - 50
Early seral	0 - 25

5.43 **Riparian Resource Value Rating.** A riparian resource value rating evaluates progress toward meeting site-specific management objectives. A rating system is based on site potential and management objectives for the riparian ecological site. Rating criteria will differ for a given site where management objectives differ.

Conversely, where objectives are the same or are complimentary for a given site, the same criteria could be applied. As many criteria can be applied as are deemed pertinent to the objectives of the site, though use of too many criteria may result in a loss of responsiveness in the rating system.

The following example demonstrates the development of resource rating criteria for a riparian site where the desired plant community and successional stage are known, based on studies of a comparison area. Using these criteria, the existing plant community is evaluated in terms of meeting desired objectives. Individual field offices must develop rating criteria specific to local site characteristics not clearly related to or controlled by on-site management should not be used as rating criteria.

Example

1. Riparian Ecological Site (PNC):

    Salix geyeriana/Carex rostrata

2. Objective:

    By the year 2000, improve riparian vegetation vigor on Bannack Creek to benefit cutthroat trout through (1) changing ecological status from mid-seral to PNC to provide a more diverse and stabilizing species composition; (2) increasing *Salix geyeriana* canopy cover from 5% to 35% or more; (3) reducing *Poa pratensis* (weak rooted) from 30% to 10% or less and concurrently increasing *Carex rostrata* (rhizomatous) from 20% to 40%; (4) increasing noon water surface shading during the June 1-July 1 period from 10% to 50% or more, and (5) reducing livestock trampling damage on lower streambanks from 50% to 20% or less of total bank area.

3.   Rating Criteria:

	Rating Points	Rated Score
a. *Salix* Cover		
Canopy cover +35%	4	
Canopy cover 20-34%	3	
Canopy cover 9-19%	2	
Canopy cover 1-8%	1	1
b. *Poa pratensis* Cover		
Canopy cover 1-10%	4	
Canopy cover 11-20%	3	
Canopy cover 21-30%	2	2
Canopy cover 31-40%	1	
c. *Carex rostrata* Cover		
Canopy cover +40%	4	
Canopy cover 30-39%	3	
Canopy cover 20-29%	2	2
Canopy cover 10-19%	1	
d. Water Surface Shading		
Percent +50%		
Percent 30-49%	3	
Percent 10-29%	2	
Percent 1-10%	1	1
e. Livestock trampling		
Bank Area 1-10%	4	
Bank Area 11-20%	3	
Bank Area 21-40%	2	
Bank Area +40%	1	1

Total: 7
Average: 7/5=1.4

    >3.4 = Excellent
3.0-3.4 = Good
2.5-2.9 = Fair
  <2.5 = Poor

4.   Conclusion:

The resource value rating is poor (Score 1.4) and Bannack Creek is not meeting management objectives

5.   Discussion:

Criteria such as embeddedness and sedimentation were not used in this case due to recognition of poor upstream conditions on a segment of the stream which was not within BLM jurisdiction. Emphasis was placed upon use of on-site riparian site characteristics which could be influenced by BLM programs. Emphasis was also placed upon *Salix* and *Carex* in objectives since their composition in PNC was well established in a CA, they are efficient to monitor and they play key roles in providing desired trout habitat characteristics (shading, cover, stability, etc.).

5.5 **Analysis, Interpretation, and Evaluation.** Follow-up consists of the analysis, actions, and decisions that are taken after the collection of data. Many monitoring programs fail because of inadequate follow-up. If a monitoring plan is done well, the follow-up actions required should be obvious and easy to do. Poor design of monitoring as reflected in the monitoring plan will make follow-up very difficult.

Follow-up consists of several distinct phases:

(1) Analysis, interpretation, and evaluation of data;

(2) presentation of results;

(3) modifying management; and

(4) modifying or maintaining objectives.

5.51 **Analysis Data.** Analysis consists of statistical or other method of summarizing data. The method for doing such analysis should be described in the monitoring plan prior to collection of any data. BLM Technical Reference 4400-5 provides guidance on analysis.

5.52 **Interpretation and Evaluation.** Interpretation and evaluation are more subjective processes. Interpretation requires explaining the meaning of the data, and evaluation requires the examination and judgment of the quality and significance of the information derived from the data. These processes require integrating all the available evidence from statistical analysis, direct observation, common sense, and other sources. BLM Technical Reference 4400-6 provides guidance on interpretation and evaluation.

5.53 **Modifying Management.** The basic purpose of monitoring is to determine if management is achieving the stated objectives. If the objectives are clearly stated, the monitoring design is sound, and decision thresholds have been defined, then the decision to modify or continue current management as appropriate should follow logically.

5.54 **Modifying Objectives.** In some cases, information from monitoring may indicate that the original objectives are impractical or infeasible. For example, an original objective may have been to restore cottonwood trees to a riparian area, yet 10 years of monitoring data suggest that the potential natural vegetation on the site is a tall shrub type. In such cases where original objectives are biologically infeasible, they should be modified to reflect achievable goals.

5.55 **Modifying Monitoring.** Monitoring programs or techniques may require modification in response to poor original design, management changes, changes in management objectives, or many other factors.

Literature Cited

BAKER, F. 1925. Aspen in the central Rocky Mountain region. U.S. Dep. Agric.Bulletin 1291, Washington, DC. 47pp.

BARBOUR, M.G., J.H. Burke, and W.D. Pitts. 1980. Terrestrial plant ecology. Benjamin/Cummins Publ. Co., Menlo Park, CA. 604pp.

BATSON, F.T., P.E. Cuplin, W.A. Crisco. 1987. The Use of Aerial Photography to Inventory and Monitor Riparian Areas. USDI, BLM, Tech. Ref. 1737-2. 13pp.

BENTLY, J.R., D.W. Seegrist, and D.A. Blakeman. 1970. A technique for sampling low shrub vegetation by crown volume classes. U.S. Dep. Agric., For. Serv., Research Note PSN-215. 11pp.

BOEHNE, P. and R. House. 1983. Stream ordering; A tool for land managers to classify western Oregon streams. U.S. Dep. Inter. Bur. Land Manage. Tech. Note OR-3. Oregon State Office Portland, OR 6pp.

BOWERS, W., W. Hosford, A. Oakley, and C. Bond. 1979. Native trout. U.S. Dep. Agric., For. Serv., General Tech. Rept. PNW-124. 16pp.

BRINSON, M.M., B.L. Swift, R.C. Plantico, and J.S. Barclay. 1981. Riparian ecosystems: Their ecology and status. U.S. Dep. Inter., Fish and Wildlife Service, Biological Services Program, FWS/OBS-81/17.

BRYANT, F.C. and M.M. Kothmann. 1979. Variability in predicting edible browse and crown volume. Journal of Range Management. 32:144-146.

CANFIELD, R.H. 1942. Sampling ranges by the line intercept method. U.S. Dep. Agric. For. Serv., Southwestern For. and Range Exp. Sta., Report No. 4.

CHOW, U.I. (editor). 1964. Handbook of Applied Hydrology. McGraw-Hill Co., New York, NY.

COLE, G.F. 1958. Range survey guide. Montana Fish and Game Dept. Booklet 18pp.

COOPERRIDER, A.Y., R.J. Boyd, and H.R. Stuart (eds). 1986. Inventory and monitoring of wildlife habitat. U.S. Dep. Inter., Bur. Land Manage., Denver Service Center, Denver, CO. 858pp.

CROUSE, M.R., and R.R. Kindschy. 1981. A method for predicting riparian vegetation potential of semi-arid rangelands. Pages 110-116 in: Symposium on Acquisition and Utilization of Aquatic Habitat Inventory Information, Western Division American Fisheries Society. Portland, OR.

CUMMINS, K.W. 1962. An evaluation of some techniques for the collection and analysis of benthic samples with special emphasis on lotic waters. The American Midland Naturalist. 67(2):477-504.

CUPLIN, P., W.S. Platts, O. Casey, and R. Masinton. 1985. A comparison of riparian area ground data with large-scale air photo interpretation. Pages 67-68 in: Riparian Ecosystems and Their Management: Reconciling Conflicting Uses. First North American Riparian Conference, Tucson, AZ U.S. Dep. Agric., For. Serv., General Tech. Report RM-120.

DASMANN, W.P. 1951. Some deer range survey methods. California Fish and Game. 37(1):43-52.

DAUBENMIRE, R. 1959. A canopy-coverage method of vegetation analysis. Northwest Sci. 33:43-64.

————. 1968. Plant communities - a textbook of synecology. Harper and Row, Publishers, New York, NY. 300pp.

DICK-PEDDIE, W.A., and J.P. Hubbard. 1977. Classification of riparian vegetation. Symposium on the importance, preservation, and management of the riparian habitat. Tucson, AZ. July 9.

ELMORE, W. 1987. Riparian Management Specialist. BLM, Prineville, Oregon. Personal Communication.

ESHELMAN, K., S. Hudson, B. Mitchell, M. Pellant, and K. Thomas. Revised 1986. The lighter side of statistics, USDI, BLM, Denver Service Center, CO 31pp.

GILLILAND, J.H. (ed). 1969. Proceedings Canadian Hydrology Symposium No. 7, Victoria, British Columbia. National Research of Canada, Subcommittee on Hydrology. Vol. 1:35-37.

GYSEL, L.W. and L.J. Lyon. 1980. Habitat analysis and evaluation. Pages 305-327 in: Schemnitz, S.C. (ed.) Wildlife Management Techniques Manual, 4th Edition. The Wildlife Society. Washington, DC.

HART, R. 1984. Evaluation of methods for sampling vegetation and delineating wetlands transition zones in coastal West-Central Florida, Jan. 1979-May 1981. Pre. For. Office, Chief of Engineers, U.S. Army, Washington, DC 20314. Contract No. DAC W39-78-C-0099. Tech. Report Y-84-2.

HELM, W.T. (ed). 1985. Glossary of stream habitat terms. Western Division, American Fisheries Society. 34pp.

HOFFER, P.M. 1962. Regime of incoming and net radiation in relation to certain parameters of density in lodgepole pine stands. PhD. dissertation. Colorado State Univ., Fort Collins, CO. 130 pp.

JACKSON, W.L., S. Hudson, and K. Gebhardt. 1985. Considerations in rangeland watershed monitoring. U.S. Dep. Inter. Bur. Land Manage. Tech. Note No. 369. 25pp.

JONES, J.R., and G.A. Schier, 1985. Growth. Pages 19-24 in: DeByle, N.V. and R.P. Winokur (ed.) Aspen: Ecology and management in the Western U.S. USDA, For. Serv., General Tech. Rep. RM-119. 283pp.

JONES, J. 1967. Environmental conditions and their relationship to aspen height growth in the So. Rocky Mts. PhD dissertation. Colorado State Univ., Fort Collins, CO. 198pp.

KELLERHALS, R., M. Church, and D.I. Bray. 1976. Classification and analysis of river processes. Journal of Hydraulics Division, ASCE. 102:813-829.

LEMMON, P.E. 1956. A spherical densiometer for estimating forest overstory density. For. Sci. 2:314-320.

LONNER, T. 1972. Age distributions and some relationships of key browse plants on big game ranges in Montana. Montana Dept. of Fish, Wildlife, and Parks, Job Final Rpt., Project No. W-120-R-2-3.

LYON, L.J. 1968. Estimating twig production of serviceberry crown volumes. J. Wildl. Manage. 32:115-118.

M'CLOSKEY, R.T., and B. Fieldwick. 1975. Ecological separation of sympatric rodents. J. Mammal. 56(1):119-129.

MACARTHUR, R.H., and J.W. MacArthur. 1961. On bird species diversity. Ecology. 42(3):594-600.

MYERS, L. 1981. Grazing on stream riparian habitats in southwestern Montana Proceedings of the Montana Chapter, Wildlife Society, Great Falls, MT.

MYERS, L. 1987. Riparian inventory and monitoring. Montana BLM Riparian Tech. Bulletin No. 1 (Revised Dec., 1987).

NEIMAN, K.E., Jr. 1977. Relationships of canopy volume, biomass, and utilization form class to annual production of *Amelanchier alnifolia*. M.S. Thesis (Range Management), Washington State Univ., Pullman, WA. 35pp.

NORTON, B.E., J. Tuhy, S. Jenson, and R. Young. 1981. An approach to classification of riparian vegetation. National Workshop on In-Place Resources Inventories: Principles and Practices. Univ. of Maine, Orono.

NUDDS, T.D. 1977. Quantifying the vegetative structure of wildlife cover. Wildlife Soc. Bull. 5(3):113-117.

PARSONS, S. and S. Hudson. 1985. Channel cross-section surveys and data analysis. U.S. Dep. Inter Bur. Land Manage. Tech. Reference TR-4341-1. 48pp.

PARSONS, T.E., J.A. Derby, and C.E. Conrad. 1982. A vegetation classification system for use in California: its conceptual basis. U.S. Dep. Agric., For. Serv., General Tech. Rept. PSW-63.

PEEK, J.M. 1970. Relationship of canopy area and volume to production of three woody species. Ecology. 51:1098-1101.

PFANKUCH, D.J. 1975. Stream reach inventory and channel stability evaluation. Pub. No. Ri-75-002, U.S. Dep. Agric., For. Serv., Northern Region, Missoula, MT. 26 pp.

PLATTS, W.S., S.F. Megahan, and G.W. Minshall. 1983. Methods for evaluating stream, riparian, and biotic conditions. U.S. Dep. Agric., For. Serv., General Tech. Rept. INT-138. 70 pp.

PLATTS, W.S., C. Armour, G.D. Booth, M. Bryant, J.L. Bufford, P. Cuplin, S. Jensen, G.W. Lienkaemper, G.W. Minshall, S.B. Monsen, R.L. Nelson, J.R. Sadell, and J.S. Tuhy. 1987. Methods for evaluating riparian habitats with application to management. USDA, For. Serv. General Tech. Report, INT-221. 177pp.

PONCE, S.L. 1981. Water quality management program. U.S. Dep. Agric., For. Serv. Tech. Paper WSDG-TP-00002. 66pp.

RANGE INVENTORY AND STANDARDIZATION COMMITTEE. 1983. Report on guidelines and terminology for range inventories and monitoring. Range Inventory and Standardization Committee (RISC), Society for Range Management. Presented to Board of Directors, SRM, Albuquerque, NM.

RECHER, S.L. 1981. Bird species diversity and habitat diversity in Australia and North America. Am. Nat. 103(1):75-80.

ROSGEN, D.L. 1985. A stream classification system. Pages 91-95. in: Riparian Ecosystems and Their Management; Reconciling Conflicting Uses. First North American Riparian Conference, Tucson, AZ. U.S. Dep. Agric., For. Serv., General Tech. Rept. RM-120.

SCHUMM, S.A. (editor). 1977. Drainage basin morphology. Dowden, Hutchinson, and Ross, Inc., Stroudsburg, PA. 352pp.

STRICKLER, G.R. and F.W. Stearns. 1962. in: Range research methods, a symposium. Denver, CO. U.S. Dep. Agric., For. Serv., Misc. Publ. No. 940.

SURBER, E.W. 1936. Rainbow trout and bottom fauna production in one mile of stream. American Fisheries Soc. Trans. 66:193-202.

USINGER, R.L. 1956. Aquatic insects of California. Univ. of Calif. Press 508pp.

U.S. DEPARTMENT OF AGRICULTURE. 1976. National range handbook. SSM-430-V. Soil Conserv. Serv. Washington, DC. 20013 143pp.

————. 1981. Soil survey manual SSM-430-V. Soil Conserv. Serv. Washington, DC. 20013 143pp.

————. 1983. National soils handbook. NSH-430-VI. Soil Conserv. Serv. Washington, DC 20013.

————. 1985. Hydric soils of the United States. National Tech. Comm. for Hydric Soils. Soil Conserv. Serv. Washington, DC 20013 173pp.

————. 1988. Integrated riparian evaluation guide (Draft). For. Serv., Intermountain Region. Ogden, UT.

U.S. DEPARTMENT OF THE INTERIOR. 1980. Wildlife and Riparian sections - Mountain Foothills EIS. Bur. Land Manage., Billings, MT. 271pp.

————. 1981. National range handbook. Bur. Land Manage. Manual H-4410-1. Washington, DC.

————. 1985a. Riparian aquatic information data summary (RAIDS). Bur. Land Manage., Div. of Resources, Denver Service Center, Denver, CO. 35pp.

————. 1985b. Rangeland monitoring: Trend studies. Bur. Land Manage. TR 4400-4. Division of Resources, Denver Service Center, Denver, CO. 130pp.

————. 1986. Wetland plants of the U.S. Fish and Wildl. Serv., Wetland Ecology Group. National Wetlands Inventory. St. Petersburg, FL. pp.

VAN HAVEREN, B.P. and W.L. Jackson. 1986. Concepts in stream riparian rehabilitation. Trans. Am. Wildl. and Nat. Resour. Conf. 51:280-289.

WILLIAMS, O. and R.B. Thomas. 1984. Guidelines for collection and analysis of sediment data. U.S. Dep. Agric., For. Serv. WSDG Draft Report. 108pp.

ZAMORA, B.A. 1981. An approach to plot sampling for canopy volume in shrub communities. Journal of Range Management. 34(2):155-156.

Appendix 1. Regional Plant Lists for Wetland Plants of the United States.

CODE	REGION	STATE COMPOSITION
1	Northeast	ME, NH, VT, MA, CT, RI, WV, KY, NY, PA, NJ, MD, DE, VA, OH
2	Southeast	NC, SC, GA, FL, TN, AL, MS, LA, AR
3	North Central	MO, IA, MN, MI, WI, IL, IN
4	North Plains	ND, SD, MT (Eastern), WY (Eastern)
5	Central Plains	NE, KS, CO (Eastern)
6	South Plains	TX, OK
7	Southwest	AZ, NM
8	Intermountain	NV, UT, CO (Western)
9	Northwest	WA, OR, ID, MT (Western), WY (Western)
0	California	CA
A	Alaska	AK
C	Caribbean	BQ (U.S. Miscellaneous Caribbean Islands) PR (Puerto Rico, AQ (Swan Islands), CZ (Canal Zone), VI (U.S. Virgin Island)
H	Hawaii	HI, AQ (American Samoa), GU (Guam), JQ (Johnston Atoll), MQ (Midway Islands), YQ (Ryukyu Islands Southern), TQ (Trust territories of the Pacific Islands), IQ, (U.S. Miscellaneous Pacific Islands), WQ (Wake Island)

To obtain copies of regional reports, please contact:

Porter B. Reed, Jr.
Wetland Ecology Group
U.S. Fish and Wildlife Service
Monroe Building, Suite 101
9720 Executive Center Drive
St. Petersburg, FL 33702

FTS 8-826-3867
Commercial 813-893-3867

69

Appendix 2. Field Form Examples*

Each State needs to take these examples and adjust them to their needs or develop their own forms.

A. EXTENSIVE STREAM RIPARIAN INVENTORY

Stream:_____ Date: _____ Observer: _____

SWA:_____ Legal Location:_____

Allotment: _____ Flow Duration: Intermittent   Perennial

                                                 Ephemeral   Subterranean

BLM Stream Miles: _____ Stream Order:_____ Landform: _____

Upstream Elevation: _____ Downstream Elevation:_____

Streambank Soil Texture: _____   Bank Rock Fragments:
                                                (greater than 15%)

Soil Reaction: _____ Gravel   Cobble   Stones   Non-Saline

Soil Wetness: Wet   Drained Soil Salinity: Saline   Non-Saline

Channel Gradient: _____% Valley Width:_____ Cross Valley Slope:_____

Channel Sinuosity: _____

Channel Confinement: Occasionally   Frequently   Confined   Entrenched

Channel Entrenchment: Aggrading   Equilibrium   Party Entrenched   Entrenched

Lateral Movement: None   Avulsion   Downcutting and Widening   Progression

Streamflow: low _____ high _____ cfs/gpm _____ Streamflow Regulation:_____

Vegetation Series: _____ Est. Canopy Cover Dominant Species:_____

Supplemental Condition Rating:

Soil Alteration Rating: Vegetation Bank Protection:

Subsurface Water Status: Riparian Condition Rating:

COMMENTS:

Improvement Potential:_____

Water Source: Transport   Inchannel Seeps   Lateral Seeps

Manmade Alterations: (list & map)_____

Erosion Processes: Headcutting   Gullying   Sheet Erosion   Bank Collapse
                             Livestock Trampling

Apparent Water Quality Impacts: Fecal   Algae Growth   Minerals
                                    Suspended Sediments   Trash   Mining Wastes

Vegetation Classification:

    Series:_____ Association:_____

    Phase:

        Forest (+61%)   Woodland (20-60%)

        Herbaceous:

        0-25%   26-50% 51-75%   +76%

        Woody Young-Even   Woody Young-Mixed   Woody All-Aged Mixed

        Woody Old-Even   Woody Old-Mixed

    Other: _____

50272 - 101

REPORT DOCUMENTATION PAGE	1. Report No. BLM/YA/PT-87/022+1737	2.	3. Recipient's Accession No.
4. Title and Subtitle Riparian Area Management Inventory and Monitoring Riparian Areas			5. Report Date July 1989
			6.
7. Author(s) Lewis H. Myers			8. Performing Organization Rept. No. TR-1737-3
9. Performing Organization Name and Address U.S. Department of the Interior Bureau of Land Management - Service Center P.O. Box 25047 Denver, CO 80225-0047			10. Project/Task/Work Unit No.
			11. Contract(C) or Grant(G) No. (C) (G)
12. Sponsoring Organization Name and Address U.S. Department of the Interior Bureau of Land Management - Service Center P.O. Box 25047 Denver, CO 80225-0047			13. Type of Report & Period Covered
			14.

15. Supplementary Notes

16. Abstract (Limit: 200 words)

   This Technical Reference contains suggested techniques and procedures to inventory and monitor riparian areas. It will assist managers in determining their specific inventory and monitoring needs. Inventory components are shown as essential or optional. Essential components should be emphasized, but they are not required. Optional components should receive less emphasis, but they may be required to meet specific management needs.

   The extensive inventory is complete using primarily remote sensing inventory data, managers identify, characterize, and roughly classify riparian sites. A decision can then be made on priorities for intensive inventories based on resource values and sitecharacters. Low resource values and/or acceptable condition may dictate the development of maintenance objectives and the establishmnet of monitoring without the completion of an intensive inventory. High values and/or unacceptable condition would probable result in a decision to do an intensive inventory.

   Intensive inventories require detailed field examination. These data are used to classify sites in more detail, and to provide site-specific management objectives and monitoring criteria.

17. Document Analysis   a. Description

Guidelines for Inventory and Monitoring

b. Identifiers/Open-Ended Terms

Riparian area inventory
Riparian area monitoring

c. COSATI Field/Group

18. Availability Statement Release Unlimited	19. Security Class (This Report) Unclassified	21. No. of Pages 89
	20. Security Class (This Page) Unclassified	22. Price

(See ANSI-Z39.18)   See Instructions on Reverse   OPTIONAL FORM 272 (4-77)
(Formerly NTIS-35)
Department of Commerce

✿ U.S. GOVERNMENT PRINTING OFFICE: 1991 - 573-003/22010